DARKNESS AND LIGHT

Darkness and Light

The Analysis
of
Doctrinal Statements

by

Garth L. Hallett, S.J.

PAULIST PRESS
New York / Paramus / Toronto

Library of Congress Catalog Card Number: 75-21734

ISBN: 0-8091-1897-1

Published by Paulist Press
Editorial Office: 1865 Broadway, N.Y., N.Y. 10023
Business Office: 400 Sette Drive, Paramus, N.J. 07652

Printed and bound in the United States of America

CONTENTS

Be careful, therefore,
that the light in you is not darkness.
If, then, your whole body is full of light,
with no part of it in darkness,
it will be bright all over,
as when a lamp shines on you
with its brightness.

Luke 11, 35-36

Preface

"The tragedy of modern Catholic theology," writes Jan Walgrave, "which was but an aspect of the tragedy of the post-tridentine Church, consisted in its isolation from the great movement from which the contemporary age was to spring. Modern thought that shaped the world went its own way and was practically ignored by the theologians of the Catholic schools. They continued to move within the orbit of a 'perennial theology,' based on a 'perennial philosophy,' discussing the same questions in the same way, making their choice from a traditional set of conflicting opinions, and adding on occasion a new question, the terms of which had first to be fitted in with the intellectual structures of the system."[1] Many would concur in this verdict, and perhaps contrast the openness of the present with the narrowness of the past. Yet it is conceivable that future generations will have something similar to say about our own age. For strong formative currents in present-day thought go their own way, practically ignored by Catholic theologians. I have in mind especially the analytic and linguistic trends which are dominant in English-speaking lands but which are so little known or understood and hence so little heeded by theologians, especially Catholic ones. To help bridge this gap, I here ask a new question, discuss it in a new way, and offer (perforce) a new solu-

1

tion. The difficulty I foresee is that my bridge-building attempt will be viewed with suspicion from both sides, by the analytically-minded at one end of the span and by Catholic theologians at the other. For, like any would-be bridge-builder, I would leave both embankments intact: Catholic theology on the one hand and linguistic philosophy, of a late-Wittgensteinian variety, on the other. And many of those at either side of this chasm look with diffidence towards the farther bank. Thus the very mention of Wittgenstein may turn some potential readers away; for in Catholic circles the Wittgenstein of legend is better known than the real. Besides, weren't Braithwaite and van Buren Wittgensteinians, and look where they ended! So let me assure the reader in advance that he will encounter nothing here which resembles those thinkers' conclusions. And if he finds my central question troubling, because of certain associations; if my manner of treating it seems strange, so inspires some malaise; if my final solution appears alarming in its novelty, let him reflect that these are the normal sensations of one who ventures out on an intellectual bridge for the first time. Just such misgivings troubled the theologians Walgrave refers to, and, too readily heeded, enclosed them in their own too-narrow world of thought.

For the benefit of non-Catholic readers I shall add that though the focal problem I have chosen to treat is likely to interest Catholic theologians more than it does them, the majority of the points illustrated in this way are of common interest to Christian theologians, regardless of denomination.

I am very grateful to Karl Becker, S.J., and Vincent Cooke, S.J., for having read and commented on the entire manuscript of this book, and to others who read parts of it. Though I have benefited from their suggestions, the reader should not attribute my opinions, especially the mistaken ones, to them.

CHAPTER ONE

The Problem and the Procedure

If someone says, "I have two and a half friends," does that make sense? If it doesn't, then the statement is neither true nor false. Nor is its truth assured by a guarantee against error. Suppose, though, that the speaker were to explain as follows: "Well, Jim is my friend, and so is John, and so is the average man. But the average man, you know, is not a concrete individual, nor on the other hand is he nothing at all. So now you see what I meant by saying I have two friends and a half." Does that make sense? Well, the nonsense is less obvious. And it can be rendered still less evident, through a formulation like the following: "I have $\sqrt[3]{15.625}$ friends." Using a still more complex formula, one might hide the lack of meaning from all but the most competent mathematicians.

Well-disguised nonsense is more than a possibility. It is a fact of life, especially in those reaches of thought where the reasoning if not the resultant formula is tortuous and complex. It is this sort of fact which accounts in large measure for the preoccupation with meaning which characterizes contemporary thought. Though thinkers of previous centuries did not ignore questions of meaning, truth was their primary concern. But priorities have been shifting, especially in the last century. A hundred years ago, Peirce introduced a method for determining meaning and thereby started American pragmatism on its way. Then the Cambridge revolt of Russell and Moore, and later the Vienna Circle, focused attention still more sharply on problems of meaning, in lands little affected by pragmatism. In still other areas, where linguistic and analytic philosophy had smaller influence, the phenomenological method resulted in a similar bracketing of theory till content was clarified.

Theologians, aware of this general movement, have sought to come abreast of the times. They mention language more frequently; attend somewhat more, perhaps, to questions of sense; apply the results and techniques of Oxonians, structuralists and others. Yet, as might have been expected, the trend which is just cresting in philosophy has yet to reach full strength in theology. In particular, whereas philosophers are generally aware that the "linguistic turn" is principally a matter of method, too many theologians still confuse linguistic philosophy with the philosophy of language, and so fail to realize that the methods used by linguistic philosophers in their study of man, morals, religion, science, history, and so on, are equally applicable and necessary in theology as a whole and not just when questions of language arise. I shall not here argue the case for their relevance, but hope to illustrate it.

The Problem

The focal purpose of this book is to fill a more limited gap, one which reveals with special clarity how incomplete the penetration of linguistic awareness has been. To the interest in truth which dominated nearly two millennia of theological thinking there corresponds a full discussion and a final definition: the doctrine of infallibility. On the corresponding question with regard to meaning there has not even been a debate. In fact, the issue has not even been formulated. I, at least, have seen no article or book which asked, much less developed and discussed, this question: *To what extent is the meaningfulness of magisterial statements guaranteed by the fact that they are magisterial statements?* Nor have I met anyone who could refer me to such a discussion.

Notice that the problem which I propose to treat is a theological one, in the area of ecclesiology, and not merely philosophical. Obviously many of the statements whose meaningfulness has been debated in philosophical circles are identical with or similar to statements found in magisterial documents; so the debates have, in a sense, dealt with the question whether and to what extent the meaningfulness of magisterial statements is guaranteed. But they have treated the question piecemeal and indirectly, not formally. And the discussions have been philosophical, not theological. It is the theological query which is new and the theological inquiry which remains to be undertaken. For of course a discussion in the Vienna Circle concerning the meaningfulness of theological statements, magisterial ones included, is no more a theological treatment of the matter than a discussion of their truth, in the same quarter, would constitute a theological treatment of infallibility.

In a certain sense of "meaning" or "significance", it is true, theologians as well as philosophers, especially of late, have shown interest in the meaningfulness of this or that point of doctrine or of dogma in general. The trend I have in mind has many spokesmen, but perhaps none clearer than William James. "If theological ideas prove to have a value for concrete life," said he, "they will be true, for pragmatism, in the sense of being good for so much."[1] Transpose this into the semantic key, via the familiar correlation between truth and meaning, and you get: "If theological ideas prove to have importance for life—negative or positive—they will be meaningful, significant." This step James in fact took. "If," for instance, "we apply the principle of pragmatism to God's metaphysical at-

tributes, strictly so called, as distinguished from his moral attributes, I think that, even were we forced by a coercive logic
to believe them, we still should have to confess them to be des-
titute of all intelligible significance."[2]

Significance in this sense is a perfectly legitimate concern,
but it is not the only one, nor is it mine in this book. I am concerned with the *what* of revelation and Church teaching, not
the *why*; with its content, not its "relevance". For the question
of content is very relevant.[3] Relevance cannot be judged apart
from content, whereas content can and must be judged apart
from relevance. The question of meaning in the primary sense
of the word, on which I shall focus, is thus the more fundamental one.

To state the contrast in James's own terms and by means of
his examples: my interest is not in the effects belief may or
may not have on people's lives, but in what they would believe
if "forced by a coercive logic", and whether there would be
anything to believe. If I believe that Admiral Byrd once made a
polar expedition, or that the earth is hot in the center, these
beliefs may have no effect whatever on my life, but there is no
doubt that, in the ordinary sense of the expression, these two
propositions do have "intelligible significance". This is the sort
of significance on which I shall focus. It is meaning in this
sense which may sometimes be lacking, and which magisterial
statements had better have if they are to teach anything at all.
And it is the guarantee of *such* meaning which theologians
have not yet seriously considered.

The situation is understandable, whichever theological camp
one considers. Some theologians take an attitude akin to that
of James: "The whole function of philosophy ought to be to
find out what definite difference it will make to you and me, at
definite instants of our life, if this world-formula or that world-
formula be the true one."[4] Others, concerned with cognitive
content, have had their hands full with the blanket, basic
charge that theological statements are void of factual meaning.
In the midst of such a debate they have not stopped to draw

distinctions, but have countered the general accusation with an equally general defense. Told that theological statements are meaningless they have roundly replied that they are meaningful.

To acknowledge that though theological statements are not all meaningless some may be and probably are, would be rather feeble apologetics, but the honest truth. However, till now theologians have generally envisaged only two possibilities: any statement or doctrine they considered, whether in a magisterial document or the writings of a fellow theologian, they have usually presumed to be either true or false. The line might be hard to draw, and the meaning be difficult to determine, but *some* meaning the statement surely had. And wherever there is meaning, there must be truth or falsehood. In their practice, if not in explicit theory, *non datur tertium*. The message of the present work, specifically with regard to magisterial statements, is: *datur tertium*.

Coming from someone who is not primarily a theologian, this assessment of the historical situation may give offense. So let me add that I feel sure there must have been some theologians in the past who considered the question of meaningfulness, and that there are more today, especially among natural theologians in dialogue with positivistic thinkers. But the references that have been provided me, in answer to my claim of general neglect, have invariably led not to counter-instances, but to traditional discussions of what some statement or doctrine meant, not whether it had any meaning at all. And since these references came from competent theologians, better acquainted than I with the relevant literature, this outcome seems significant. It indicates how rare the exceptions must be. And it suggests that the question I am raising is so unfamiliar even to present-day theologians that they find it difficult to grasp just what the issue is.

So let me illustrate the point by means of one of the references given me. I was told that I would find the question of meaningfulness raised in a discussion of *Humanae Vitae* by

Philippe Delhaye.[5] Here, instead, is what I found. Expressions such as "intrinsically wrong", the author observes, are not employed in a single, invariant sense.[6] In the discussions of the pontifical commission, for instance, prior to the encyclical's issuance, two quite different meanings appeared: whereas some used the expression to qualify a deed "on the psychological level, that is, as an act which has a certain significance through its insertion in a human context", others used it in reference to "an act in its sheer materiality".[7] So with regard to contraception, "let us ask in what sense HV calls it intrinsically wrong. Most of the episcopal texts studied here undoubtedly take it as wrong in the moral sense. . . . But is every other interpretation excluded? Mightn't we suppose that the condemnation is aimed at contraception taken as a material fact prior to its insertion into a human context?"[8] Delhaye's conclusion is that we might. But notice now that had he been interested in meaningfulness, this conclusion would have been the start of his discussion, not its end. Noting the two divergent readings actually given and the reasons that might be cited in favor of each, he would have questioned whether either interpretation could reasonably be presented as the correct one, to the exclusion of the other. If it couldn't, a negative verdict on meaningfulness would appear likely. For certainly the encyclical does not have both senses, and if it has neither of these two most plausible ones, then it probably has none. That is how the question of meaningfulness would have shaped up. However, nothing of the kind appears in Delhaye's discussion; his interest lies elsewhere. I do not say this in criticism. My aim is to illustrate the distinction between traditional concern about meaning and the neglected question of meaningfulness. How completely this latter is excluded from the mental horizon of most theologians appears from the fact that this and similar writings were cited to me, by theologians, as evidence of theologians' awareness of the problem.

This lack of concern about meaningfulness is mirrored and partially explained by typical objections against my proposed inquiry. One reaction is to reply that *of course* magisterial statements are meaningful. I have also been told that, strictly speaking, statements do not mean anything; only people do. And the authors of magisterial statements surely meant *something* by them. A reader who has such difficulties with my proposed problem, judging it no problem at all but a confusion or mistake, is not likely to read very far. And such difficulties, I have found, are common. So I had better consider them, at least briefly, here at the start.

"My basic problem with your position," wrote one prominent theologian, after reading an earlier version of this chapter, "relates to the meaning of meaning. You seem to think that sentences as such 'mean'. I would say people mean, or may mean, things by sentences. *Actiones sunt suppositorum.*" A number of unexamined suppositions, it seems to me, lurk beneath these words (suppositions not confined to Scholastic thinking, as the closing sentence might suggest). One wonders, especially, whether the familiar use of the words "mean" and "meaning" in the English language has been taken into account, then rejected as mistaken, or whether it has simply been ignored. For English-speakers in general, and not just philosophers of some particular school, say such things as: "These two propositions have a different meaning," "Sentences in different languages may have the same meaning," "I did not grasp the meaning of his words straight off," "The original meaning of the text is not easy to discern," "A rhetorician is more concerned with the sound of his statements than with their meaning." Such is common usage. And can usage be *wrong*? By what standard, how established? Surely it is the current use of terms which determines correctness (I do not say "truth") and confers on most words, including the word "meaning", whatever sense they possess. So where is the error in saying that statements have meaning?

According to a primitive conception of language and thought, people perform meaning-acts which confer meaning on their words. The meaning never leaves the mind to reside in the words (how could it, since the meaning is spiritual and the words are material?). Hence only by extrinsic denomination do we call statements, sentences, propositions, and the like meaningful. It is somewhat as when we say something is seen, or is visible; the seeing is in us, not in the object, and so is the capacity for sight. Now most philosophers who attend to the way words are actually employed would agree, I imagine, that this "meaning act" is what Wittgenstein termed a grammatical fiction.[9] Of course there are mental acts, for instance the act of imagining a person's appearance or calculating a square root in one's head. But in the sense in which these are acts, meaning is not an act (nor, for that matter, is believing, judging, knowing, etc.). To assert an "act" as the referent of every psychological verb would void the term "act" of meaning and be thoroughly misleading. It would be as though, after referring in the normal way to the acts of opening a book or lighting a pipe, one were to argue that growing up, growing a beard, growing potatoes, and growing tired are likewise "bodily acts".

I shall not dwell on this point. For others have made it fully, and I can refer the reader to their treatments.[10] Besides, the basic difficulty for my proposal may remain even when belief in a meaning act is abandoned. As we call a gift generous, it may be said, because of the *giver's* generosity, yet do not identify his generosity as an act, so we may call a statement meaningful because of the speaker's meaning without identifying that as an act. And were this quite generally the case—did sentences and statements "as such" have no meaning—it would follow that any words a person speaks are meaningful provided *he* means something by them, and that whatever he means by them is what they mean. However, this doctrine of purely extrinsic denomination is contradicted by the fact that we sometimes do term a person's utterance meaningless even though he meant something by it, or judge that a person meant one thing and his words meant another. Consider, for instance, the case of the Austrian lady who learned her English from mischievous friends during her first voyage to the United States. Arriving at the ballroom door one evening in company with a bishop, she stepped aside, and with a gesture towards the entrance said sweetly: "Scram, your excellency!" We know what she meant, but it isn't what her words meant. Or at least that is one natural way of expressing the situation.[11]

However, some people, influenced perhaps by the verbal parallel between "mean" with a personal subject and "mean" with an impersonal subject, might claim that the lady's words, and not only she, meant: "After you, your excellency." And if such assessments are common, they form a conflicting usage. And usage determines correctness. So who is right?

Most non-technical concepts are vague and fluctuating at the borders (that is, with respect to non-standard cases like the lady at the door); and semantic terms such as "meaning" and "meaningful" are notably imprecise. After all, precise, constant discriminations concerning the complicated workings of language can hardly be expected of the general public, and philosophers have vigorously tugged and stretched these terms in many directions. Thus I can understand the puzzlement of some when they hear the suggestion that magisterial statements may occasionally be meaningless. Surely, they feel, such pronouncements must have meaning in *some* sense of the word "meaning". I shall not contest this, but shall only observe that if it is thus that meaning is assured to magisterial statements— not in virtue of their intelligibility, but by the elasticity of the concept "meaning"—then the guarantee has little significance. If semantic terms like "meaning" and "meaningful" are applicable to any statement, no matter how incoherent, provided the incoherence is somewhat camouflaged, then I shall have to seek other means with which to state pointedly and discuss precisely the problem I have roughly described as one concerning the meaningfulness of magisterial statements.

The Procedure

In such a situation the Wittgensteinian technique of language-games seems best. "If we want to study the problems of truth and falsehood," said Wittgenstein, "of the agreement and disagreement of propositions with reality, of the nature of assertion, assumption, and question, we shall with great advantage look at primitive forms of language in which these forms of thinking appear without the confusing background of highly complicated processes of thought. When we look at such simple forms of language the mental mist which seems to enshroud our ordinary language disappears. We see activities, reactions, which are clear-cut and transparent. On the other hand we recognize in these simple processes forms of language not separated by a break from our more complicated ones. We see that we can build up the complicated forms from the primitive ones by gradually adding new forms."[12] Transposed to the present situation, where the contrast required is no longer between "primitive forms" and "our ordinary use of language", but between simple samples of ordinary use and complex theological ones, the methodological proposal can be reworded as follows: "If we want to study the problems of infallibility and irreformability, of the agreement of magisterial statements with Scripture and tradition, of the nature of revelation, faith, and mystery, of the various levels of meaning found in Scripture or degrees of meaningfulness in the documents of councils and popes, we shall with great advantage look at simpler forms of everyday speech and life in which kindred questions arise without the confusing background of theological debate. When we look at such simple paradigms the mental mist which seems to enshroud the theological questions dissipates. We note simple, basic aspects of human thought and language which are relatively clear-cut and transparent. On the other hand we recognize in these simple processes forms of life not separated by a break from the more complicated ones; what we learn from them applies to the others too."

Behind this unfamiliar method in theology lies a deep mistrust of *a priori* laws and generalizations, of theories, theses, and definitions, arising from repeated recognition that they usually turn out to be either false, or misleading, or tautological, or ultimately incoherent. I favor an end to such proclamations as the verification principle of the logical positivists, or Wittgenstein's early pronouncements that language consists entirely of propositions and that all propositions are logical pictures. Theologians too have frequently manifested an unhealthy craving for generality, not perceiving perhaps that there is a middle way between theories and a mere thicket of particular facts.

One alternative is the method of ordered models suggested in Wittgenstein's *Philosophical Investigations* and exemplified most fully in his *Brown Book*. "Our clear and simple language-games," he said, "are not preparatory studies for a future regularization of language—as it were first approximations, ignoring friction and air-resistance. The language-games are rather set up as *objects of comparison* which are meant to throw light on the facts of our language by way not only of similarities, but also of dissimilarities."[13] In like manner, the samples I shall offer from ordinary discourse will not serve as the basis for eventual theories or theses (at least of the ordinary, "scientific" sort), nor will they be applied willy-nilly to complex theological cases, as though there were no differences. Rather, the method of models is intended as an antidote to hasty theorizing. Lack of such clear-cut, simple paradigms, or rather of reflection on them, has led even linguistic philosophers to unrealistic contrasts between theological and non-theological discourse, to the detriment of the former, or, on the other hand, to dangerously reductive assimilations of theological discourse to non-theological. Sometimes far-reaching proposals are made concerning revelation, development of doctrine, or infallibility as a result of misunderstandings which examination of the simplest paradigms might have remedied. Thus I would make the prayer of Augustine my own, and recommend it as a motto for this whole inquiry: "God grant to men to see in a small thing notices common to things both great and small."[14]

Lest I violate my own principles at the start, by remaining general and abstract, let me illustrate my meaning concretely and thereby demonstrate the kind of utility concrete examples may have. I hope Anselm Atkins will not be offended if I start with a negative sample, recommended both by its clarity and by its general relevance in a study such as this, chosen from his writings. In a treatment of magisterial statements he reasons as follows:

A form of words can symbolize "an indefinite number of diverse propositions". Language is ambiguous, and many propositions can "fit the same verbal phraseology". Thus, "Caesar has crossed the Rubicon," a form of words, may differ, as a proposition, for the Roman legionnaire, the British historian, or the American schoolboy, depending on what each has in mind by "Caesar". Now the question can be raised whether an anathema is directed against a verbal statement or against one or more of the propositions which it might embody. Since a given unorthodox opinion (proposition) can be expressed in many ways, it would be highly improbable if the anathema were directed solely against the mere external phraseology of the opinion and not against the opinion itself, regardless of its phraseology. I take it, then, that an anathema contradicts a proposition rather than the "form of words" in which it happens to be expressed. But, returning to the notion that a form of words may embody many propositions, does the anathema contradict one, or several, or all of the possible propositions into which the verbal statement can be analyzed? In order for the anathema itself to be true—and the irrevisability of conciliar canons is apparently an irrevisable tenet of Roman Catholicism—at least *one* of the condemned propositions must be false. Since for the most part the propositions into which the condemned statement is analyzable will be significantly similar, common sense suggests that *many* of them will lie within the range of meaning of the condemned statement. But it is not logically necessary that *all* the propositions into which the condemned statement is analyzable are false. The most an anathema *need* say is that a certain verbal statement is analyzable into at least *one* false proposition.[15]

As Atkins employs the word "statement", his references to "propositions into which a statement is analyzable" could indicate (for instance) either the different meanings an identical set of words might have for an identical hearer on different occasions and in different contexts, or the different meanings a sentence might have in a single setting for varied hearers. Since the latter alternative differs so radically from the former, and seems the most relevant in the discussion of a single magisterial utterance, and is the one indicated by Atkins' example, I shall focus on it.

Atkins recognizes that "for the most part the propositions into which the condemned statement is analyzable will be significantly similar." Thus the point of his comparison is not that for one person "Caesar crossed the Rubicon" might mean simply "The conqueror of Gaul crossed the Rubicon," for another "The first Roman emperor crossed the Rubicon," for another "The husband of Calpurnia crossed the Rubicon," and so on, and that the falsehood of one of these is compatible with the truth of all the rest. He realizes that for each individual the content would be more complex, and that for any two individuals some elements would probably be common. Thus it is likely that he was influenced by thoughts such as those expressed in number 79 of Wittgenstein's *Philosophical Investigations*. Each person, Wittgenstein observes, if asked to say who Moses was, or who Caesar was, would give a somewhat different description. No one item, furthermore, is considered essential, even by the person who lists it; upon learning that the man we had in mind did not capture Vercingetorix or was not stabbed by Brutus we do not conclude that Caesar never existed. The content of the sign "Caesar" forms a mobile cluster, far more mobile in fact than the ordinary concept. Thus Atkins' example, employing two proper names rather than general terms, is already suspect. But even this atypical example provides no support for his proposals.

For consider how the statement "Caesar crossed the Rubicon" might be analytically restated according to such personal variations in content: "The Roman general who conquered Gaul and courted Cleopatra and was stabbed by Brutus crossed the Rubicon"; "The Roman general who conquered Gaul and captured Vercingetorix and ended the Roman republic crossed the Rubicon"; "The Roman general who conquered Gaul and captured Vercingetorix and was stabbed by Brutus crossed the Rubicon"; etc. Now which of these propositions does a person deny when he denies that Caesar crossed the Rubicon? On any occasion for which the preceding analysis was relevant, the declaration "Caesar did *not* cross the Rubicon" would negate them all. And if some hearer's notion of Caesar was odd enough to escape elimination—if, for instance, he supposed that Caesar Augustus was meant—we would not include that idiosyncratic content among the "propositions into which the statement is analyzable". He would simply be mistaken about the statement's meaning.

No one, I imagine, will argue with this verdict. And obviously it was more in accord with Atkins' suggestion to do as I did and slice up the subject term rather than the predicate. The reader may wonder, though, what the result would be if instead of a proper name we considered a general term, and instead of analyzing the subject we turned to the predicate. It is defective predicates, after all, which generally decide the falsehood of propositions. And general terms like "grace", "person", and "sacrament" predominate in magisterial statements, rather than fluctuating historical names such as "Caesar". What, then, does the typical case look like?

Still more clearly opposed to Atkins' suggestion. Consider for instance the statement "My car is red." As I shall explain more fully in the next chapter (#2), in terms of its informative power this statement is equivalent to a disjunction, listing different shades of red: "My car is crimson or scarlet or rose or salmon or. . . ." In accordance with Atkins' remark about analysis into component *propositions*, we might expand the translation: "My car is crimson, or my car is scarlet, or my car is rose, or my car is salmon, or. . . ." Since any one of these colors verifies the general statement, the negation of the general statement eliminates each of them. It negates every one of the component propositions. Thus whereas the positive assertion might be analyzed into a series of positive propositions in disjunction, as above, its negation would take the form of a logical product, in which each member is negated: "My car is not crimson and my car is not scarlet and my car is not carmine and. . . ." This result, too, is hardly debatable. Close examination of even one typical negation, such as "My car is not red," would have revealed the difficulties in Atkins' sweeping proposal.

Very simple models, therefore, may have great therapeutic utility and illuminative power. For instance, once we recognize that all statements contain at least one vague term, we realize that the disjunctive pattern of "My car is red" typifies assertions, and the conjunctive pattern of "My car is not red" characterizes negations. The lesson carries far. But suppose we tried to turn this insight into a theory or thesis, to the effect that *all* assertions and negations can be so analyzed. The only result would be endless debate and a tangle of words, resulting in the conclusion that the theory was either false or a tautology. For what would count as a negation? All and only those statements in which "not" occurs a single time? Even if we extended the list to include "non-", "no", "in-", and the like, the thesis would still not work. For the sort of switch from disjunction to conjunction typically effected by "not" is achieved by many other expressions as well, where the negation, we would say, is veiled; and the addition of "not" to such expressions reverses the sign once again, turning conjunction back into disjunction. Thus "absent" negates "present" and is itself negated by "not absent", so that the depth structure of this surface negation is just the opposite of that required by the thesis. If,

on the other hand, we simply *define* negation in terms of the
conjunctive structure discovered in "My car is not red," we
turn the theory into an uninteresting tautology; what started as
the predicate of a theory has now slipped into the subject term
as well. And in the tedious and probably polemical process of
arriving at this tautology we learn no more about negation
than we knew at the start.

Here too I have used one concrete example to illustrate a
general point. Philosophers or theologians habituated to the
search for definitions and theses, who are therefore likely to
find my discussions "vague" or "unscientific", can sense from
this one paradigm the reasons for my method. They may sense,
too, that the sort of generality aimed at in a definition or thesis
may often be more safely and clearly conveyed by means of a
well-chosen sample. And just as many individual propositions
may be put together to form an overall theory, so too a number
of samples may be arranged so as to give an overall view of the
landscape. Such is Wittgenstein's method of ordered models,
or, as he termed it, the method of "perspicuous representation"
by means of "intermediate cases". As a guide may lead a
group from one street to another and so familiarize them with
the confusing heart of some old town, so one linguistic example
may be made to overlap another till the series constitutes a trip
from end to end of some puzzling domain.

The terrain which interests us is that stretching from sure
sense to sure nonsense. We need to see what happens along the
way. So a first series of samples, in Chapter Two, starts with
clear, unproblematic statements, then passes to paradigms
which, though still simple in comparison with speculative propositions, become more and more problematic, till finally, im-
perceptibly, the border between sense and nonsense is crossed.
The purpose of the chapter, as of the following one, on moral
meaning, is to provide background for the discussion of genuine, complex cases, in Chapters Four and Five. Each down-to-
earth example in Chapter Two is intended to make one or two
points more clearly than would be possible with illustrations

drawn from philosophy or theology. However, once the points are made in this perspicuous fashion, they can then be applied to philosophical and theological cases, which, though more complex, are basically similar to the simple paradigms. Such is the program of Chapter Four, which does not, however, simply run parallel to the first series, on a deeper level, but focuses on the murky zone between sense and nonsense where doubts are most likely to arise about the meaningfulness of theoretical statements. It thus provides concrete illustrations, not just general principles, with which to work in the subsequent, fifth chapter, where an answer is finally attempted to the general question whether magisterial statements must have meaning. The final, sixth chapter will then indicate the broader significance of this one paradigm study, which is itself a sort of language-game, intrinsically interesting but still more important for its manifold implications.

CHAPTER TWO

From Meaningful to Meaningless

Although Wittgenstein is commonly considered, with reason, to be an opponent of transcendental theology, his later thought tends to eliminate two main sources of difficulty for the transcendental use of language. One is the traditional notion that the main function of communication with words is the transfer of thoughts, these thoughts being equated with the words' meanings, and these in turn with concepts, and these in turn with mental representations or likenesses. The verbal signs express the conscious contents of the speaker's mind and beget similar representations in the mind of the hearer. But whose representations can keep pace with the assertions of theology? Who can represent to himself the transcendental realities of which it speaks? Descartes, it is true, claimed to possess a positive representation of the Infinite, so rich and wonderful that God alone could have caused it. But most theologians have been more modest in their claims. So the problem naturally arises: If theological expressions do not serve to excite adequate mental representations, corresponding to the things spoken of, what is their function? How justify a use of language which differs so radically from the ordinary?

The Wittgensteinian answer is that this supposed exception is not an exception. Language never does function in the way traditionally supposed. Mental representations do of course occur while we speak, and doubtless we could not get along without them. But the representations are not meanings, nor do they adequately represent the things spoken of, nor do they accompany every word, nor do those in the mind of the reader or hearer match those in the mind of the writer or speaker, nor is the excitation of mental representations the principal function of language. Far more important is the communication of knowledge, though here too we must beware of traditional misconceptions.

Knowledge is not a conscious act or state. For knowledge is what we typical speakers of the English language call knowledge, just as chairs are what we call chairs, and we do not ordinarily use the word "knowledge", or "know", as the name for an act or conscious state. When, for instance, we ask a person whether he knows the direction to the station or whether he knows German, we are not inquiring whether he has just thought about the direction or whether the whole of German grammar and several thousand words of German vocabulary have just flashed through his mind. I need not insist on the matter, but will simply point out that it is this ordinary sense of the word "know" that I shall have in mind from now on. When I propose a cognitive analysis, I shall be suggesting what *knowledge* a person acquires from a statement (supposing it to be true), not what thoughts come to his mind. The two things are quite distinct.

The difference comes out in the criteria applied in both cases. The contents of a person's thinking are determined introspectively, by the person himself, whereas anyone can ascertain a person's knowledge, for instance by hearing him give directions to the station or seeing him lead an inquirer there. Likewise, a person's knowledge of German is established by his answering questions about German grammar and vocabulary, or simply by his speaking German. These performances, notice, are not mere clues to something inner, the actual knowledge, but are the ultimate criteria applied, on a par with falling water as a criterion of rain, or white flakes in the air as a criterion of snow.

If this distinction between thought and knowledge is not kept in mind, my analyses will appear implausible, even preposterous. For on the one hand it is the wide extent of the knowledge conveyed by a statement, as contrasted with the fragmentary thoughts it excites, which justifies emphasis on the cognitive when analyzing statements; yet it is this same discrepancy which is likely to discredit cognitive analysis in the eyes of anyone who, failing to note the distinction, equates knowledge with a conscious act and limits the meaning of words to momentary contents of consciousness. When presented with a long and complex analysis he is likely to object, "But this is absurd! Surely we don't think of all that when we hear the words!" No, but we would answer all that if asked, and such verbal expression is the foremost criterion of *knowledge*.

This first Wittgensteinian solution to the problem of transcendence, extending meaning beyond the narrow bounds of conscious representation, will be developed in the course of the present chapter. It is clarified also by his second major contribution to the problem, intimately connected with the first. I shall state this contribution in terms of analogy, understanding by that term any use of words which falls between univocity on the one hand, as traditionally conceived (roughly: the designation of common essences), and equivocity on the other (where about the only bond is the identical word). The need of analogy in this broad sense has always been recognized by theologians, but it is Wittgenstein who, more than anyone else, has vindicated it as characteristic of language as a whole and not a dubious exception.

In the opposed general view of language, thought, and the world, a one-to-one correspondence holds between words and ideas, and between ideas and things. A general term, whether verb or adverb, noun or adjective, "expresses" a specific mental content (the "idea" or "concept"), and this in turn mirrors some constant feature in reality (an "essence", "nature", "property", etc.), common to all the varied things to which the term is applied. "Thought, language, now appear to us as the unique correlate, picture, of the world. These concepts: proposition, language, thought, world, stand in line one behind the other, each equivalent to each."[1]

This grandiose but simplistic conception can be corrected by attentive examination of practically any word. Wittgenstein proposed the simple term "game", and asked: What one feature or set of features is found in all the things we call games, and found in them alone? In what does the "essence" of games consist and what, therefore, does the elusive mental representation univocally represent? His answer is well known: "We see a complicated network of similarities overlapping and criss-crossing: sometimes overall similarities, sometimes similarities of detail."[2]

"And for instance the kinds of number form a family in the same way. Why do we call something a 'number'? Well, perhaps because it has a—direct—relationship with several things that have hitherto been called number; and this can be said to give it an indirect relationship to other things we call the same name. And we extend our concept of number as in spinning a thread we twist fibre on fibre. And the strength of the thread does not reside in the fact that some one fibre runs through its whole length, but in the overlapping of many fibres."[3]

Wittgenstein did not universalize this account. There are many other conceptual patterns in language, in fact an endless variety of them. But these cases are typical, whereas essences and the "univocal" use of terms are not. Nor, therefore, are mental "concepts" or "meanings" as traditionally conceived. Once the consequences of Wittgenstein's analyses are recognized, the whole edifice of one-to-one correspondence crumbles, leaving many of the old pieces but none of the old order.

Language finally appears in all its true, mystifying complexity.

The problem of analogy, however, is clarified. From the vantage-point of Wittgenstein's analysis there emerges, in broad and general outline, the following dialectical triad, which represents no neat historical process but can be illustrated with well-known examples from the history of western thought. The thesis position, recognizing the possibility and need of analogy but regarding it as the exception, is represented by, for instance, most scholastic philosophers and theologians. Univocity is taken as the rule, but sophisticated explanations, for instance in terms of proportionality, may succeed in justifying theological expressions. Thinkers less favorably inclined to religion, or at least to theology, are likely to be less lenient towards such stretching of terms; the normal becomes the norm and analogy becomes suspect. Both positions, thesis and antithesis, war in the thought of Kant, who invoked proportionality to justify his own extension of "cause" but declared void all theological or metaphysical extensions of that and other categories beyond the limits of experience. Now, in a development both continuous and discontinuous with these antithetical positions, Wittgenstein has established analogy as the ordinary thing, thereby providing the basis for a synthetic solution. Scholastics were basically correct, we may say, in defending analogy, but undercut their own position by accepting univocity as the rule. Their opponents have been right in rejecting special privileges for theology and looking with suspicion on any sharp dichotomy between theological and other uses of terms, but have erred in supposing the ordinary uses to be rigid and uniform. By eliminating this widespread supposition, common to both proponents and opponents of theology, Wittgenstein cleared theological statements of all criticism based merely on their recourse to analogy.

Yet the problem is recast, not solved. For granted that most terms are elastic, just how far will they stretch? Granted that our use of words is freer and more varied than was commonly imagined, surely there are limits, where freedom becomes license and analogy turns into nonsense? But what shall count as sense, what as nonsense? As Wittgenstein has made clear, when a concept has fuzzy borders, as do the concepts "meaning" and "sense", to draw a sharp line and declare that on this side lies meaning and on the other nonsense is an arbitrary terminological decision with no binding power and determining no matter of fact. The only interesting thing is the distinction drawn, not the subsequent tagging. And to make the distinction, no "theory" is necessary. But examples are, so as to give clear, intelligible content to the general terms used in making the distinction; for they, too, are probably fuzzy. Such is the rationale which underlies the following examples—such the general question, and such the method. The question is the limits of sense, and the method is to line up samples, from meaningful to meaningless. Starting with expressions readily recognized as meaningful and moving to others we readily brand as nonsense, I shall note what happens along the way, especially in the no-man's land where we are at a loss what verdict to give.

1.   "Where is my math book?" asks Jim.
        "It's on the living room table," replies
        his mother.

When analyzed cognitively, the statement "It's on the living room table" turns out to be an indefinite, extremely long disjunction. The expression "on the table" covers a great many different possible positions, and the hearer does not know, in virtue of the words, either just which of these possible positions the book is in (the content is disjunctive) or just what and how many possible positions the expression covers (the disjunction is indefinite). The "cash value" of saying Jim typically acquires this indefinite *knowledge* consists, for instance, in the fact that when he enters the living room he directs his eyes to the table, and more precisely to its surface. And if his mother asks, "Did you find it there?" he will reply "Yes" if it was in any one of those indefinitely many positions within the disjunction, "No" if it was on the floor or on a chair or in any of the countless positions lying outside the disjunction.

It would therefore be equally realistic to add an endless conjunction of negations to the cognitive analysis already proposed. When he hears "It's on the living room table," Jim learns that the book is not in the kitchen nor in his bedroom nor on the living room mantlepiece, etc., etc. That this is so comes out in the fact that he goes into the living room to fetch the book, but not into the kitchen or into the bedroom, and goes to the table, not to the mantlepiece. And if you asked him whether the book was in one of these other places, he would answer "No." When I speak of his knowledge, I make no further supposition than such evident facts as these. In the ordinary sense of the words "know" and "learn", there is no doubt that the indefinite disjunction of affirmative propositions and the conjunction of negations represent what a typical hearer learns and knows in such a case.

But it would be unrealistic to suggest that even a sizeable fraction of this disjunctive and conjunctive content typically comes before his mind. He does not silently formulate all these propositions. Nor, as he walks toward the living room, does he rapidly imagine all those possible positions, on the table and off. What good would that do him? What information would it provide that the words did not? As Wittgenstein observed, "It is no more essential to the understanding of a proposition that one should imagine anything in connection with it, than that one should make a sketch from it."[4]

2.   "Whose car is that they're towing away?" Simpson asked, looking down from the office window. "Mine is red," replied Jones, worried. "You're safe, then; the one they have in tow is blue."

From the preceding analyses and discussion it should be clear why I previously suggested that the statement "My car is red" be analyzed as an indefinite disjunction. For the concept "red" resembles the expression "on" in its vagueness. A red car is either crimson or rose or carmine or salmon or scarlet or. . . . Furthermore, it is neither blue nor orange nor purple nor green nor. . . . These colors lie beyond the border, as did the chair and mantlepiece in the previous example. The legitimacy of including this conjunction of negations in the informative content of the statement "My car is red" is suggested, for instance, by the reply "You're safe, then," when Simpson saw the car was blue. He would have said the same if it were green or black, but might have hesitated about salmon pink.

For theology, special significance attaches to the fact that the content of even a homely predicate like "red" varies widely according to the background of the hearer. A small child who hears a color predication learns the mere look of the object. So did our ancestors. Then came scientific discoveries concerning the absorption, reflection, and composition of light. Now numerous hearers know that a red object is one which absorbs light of certain wave-lengths and reflects the rest. Other hearers know the precise range of wave-lengths within which red light falls. It may sound ridiculous, I know, to put all this knowledge into the cognitive content of the statement "My car is red," and in a sense it is. These words do not and cannot communicate such *general* information about red objects and red light. But anyone who possesses the general information receives much fuller specific information from the words "My car is red." If he knows the physics of light in a vague, general way, he knows that the car in question absorbs some of the light and reflects the rest. If he has more exact information, he knows the wave-lengths of the light the car reflects. Such knowledge, being particular, is not a theory, but it is theoretical.

I shall not be able to dwell on this distinction between theory and theoretical content the way it deserves, but will only point out that the pattern is universal, extending to statements and general beliefs of every category—scientific, philosophical, theological, etc.,—and is crucial for the treatment of some topics discussed by theologians, though it has seldom been noticed by them. Generally and abstractly put, the cognitive pattern is as follows: a general belief (theory, thesis, doctrine, law, etc.) plus a particular proposition produce a particular, theoretical component in the overall cognitive content of the statement. For instance, someone believes that all M are P, hears that some S is M, so believes that some S is P. Concretely: he believes, for example, that red objects (general) absorb some light and reflect the rest; hears that my car (particular) is red; so believes that my car (particular) absorbs some light and reflects the rest.

That is what he learns. But a second person learns less, a third more, always in accordance with the knowledge that each one has when he hears the statement. A whole extra dimension of disjunctive, indefinite diversity thus opens up, not within the content for any single hearer at the moment he is affected by the words, but in the population as a whole, and perhaps within the history of some one individual, if his knowledge subsequently increases and the content grows correspondingly. The original statement, if not forgotten, combines with each new theory to produce more theoretical content, not consciously, but cognitively. Though the person may not have thought since childhood of the car he heard called red, if he has studied optics since, he can now tell you, if asked, how that car reflected light. If he had never heard the statement, he could not; that is why this later knowledge might still be called the content of that statement. If, on the other hand, he did not know and understand the theory, he would neither know nor understand this later increment; that is why the added content may be called theoretical.

A new point of interest appears if we turn our attention to the subject term and examine the complex disjunctive structure of the concept "car". When I inform someone that I have a car (which I can do as effectively with a subject term as with a predicate), what sort of knowledge does he acquire? What counts as a *car*? Well, sedans and coupes, four-wheeled cars and three-wheeled, cars with motors in the front and others with the motor in the rear, large cars and small, powerful and puny, single-toned and three-toned—an endless variety, all related by what Wittgenstein called "family resemblances". But don't they all at least have a motor? Well, what of the car in Candid Camera, which rolled into a service station at the bottom of a hill? "I think there's something wrong with my motor," said the lady at the wheel; "would you take a look?" So the attendant did, to the delight of the television audience watching his expression as he lifted the hood and found—no motor. But we need not search for farfetched examples. Many an "abandoned car" along the roadside—that is, many a thing we so refer to—contains no motor.

This disjunction, then, for the expression "my car", is far more complicated than the previous two ("red" and "on the table"). Each member of the disjunction includes a different set of typical car-characteristics, enough to constitute a car. The possible combinations are endless; so, therefore, is the cognitive disjunction.

To this complexity there corresponds a multiple indefiniteness, which, in view of the guiding interest of this chapter, requires elucidation. First, though we can easily name some "family characteristics" of cars, we would be hard put to name them all. For the list has never been drawn up. Furthermore, even if we managed after long observation of usage (and many arbitrary decisions) to enumerate the characteristic features which together form the concept "car", we have no idea how many of these family traits a candidate should possess in order to qualify as a car. For this too has never been decided. And the list is not fixed once for all. And the family characteristics themselves are probably of the same sort, with only vague and fluctuating boundaries. Such is the indefiniteness and complexity of most ordinary concepts, such as "car", "book", "clothes", "game", "house", and so on. Elastic analogy is the rule.

A final point deserves mention. When we think of a word

like "car" and of the indefinite range of things it designates, we may tend to conceive the indefiniteness as a mere matter of grammar. The things themselves are known and definite. There are, for instance, four-wheeled cars, and three-wheeled cars, and three-wheeled motorcycles; and between the last two falls the indefinite borderline. We know all the referents but are vague about the word. But such is not the situation. It is important for our purposes to recognize that our knowledge gives out as well. There have been cars, are cars, and will be cars of varieties we have never encountered or conceived: cars with steam engines; cars with chains like those on bicycles; circus cars that explode; cars that split in two and proceed on their separate ways; cars like the one I shall always remember: an orange crate up front and a bathtub in the rear, where passengers reclined in state. Reality too is elastic, not just the word. But how elastic is the word?

3.   During recent years, newspapers and magazines contained frequent reports of flying saucers (*sic*) which various individuals claimed to have sighted, and of investigations which were made in an attempt to verify or falsify their claims.

It seems fairly evident why the term "saucer" was used: the alleged objects had roughly the shape of saucers. Not the size, weight, material, speed, location, construction, contents, or purpose of saucers, but just the shape. And this is worth noting. For an analysis like the preceding one, of the concept "car", might easily suggest that a new, unnamed object would have to bear a "family resemblance" to existing members of a "family" in order to merit the family name. A new-type vehicle, to be called a car, would have to possess several car characteristics; a new pastime put on sale at Christmas would have to possess several game characteristics to be called a game; and so on. Though identity of essence is not necessary, it might appear that close similarity is. For "how should we explain to someone what a game is?" asked Wittgenstein. "I imagine that we should describe *games* to him, and we might add: 'This *and similar things* are called "games".' "[5] That is, things of the same family as these, not distant cousins.

Such an interpretation of Wittgenstein and such an analysis of language would raise new problems for transcendental discourse. Theology might seem to have survived the difficulties of essentialism and representationalism only to succumb to this less stringent demand: close similarity. For crossword puzzles, it might be urged, are not called games, despite their close resemblance to anagrams, which are. Dancing resembles hopscotch just as nearly, yet it too is not a game. So how can we apply terms like "good", "wise", and "father" to God? Isn't the dissimilarity between him and his creatures immeasurably greater than that between dancing and hopscotch, or between crossword puzzles and anagrams?

Our sample corrects such thinking, and shows where the error lies. Were absolute similarity the norm for how far terms may be extended, we might argue as follows: it would be wrong to call a plate a saucer; yet a plate resembles a saucer much more closely than a flying saucer does; therefore it would be still more mistaken to call that flying object a flying saucer. But of course we do call a flying saucer a flying saucer, and experience no difficulty in communication. So what has gone wrong with this account of how language "should" work? A reply would be: The confused impression that language works by similarity was largely correct, and often the similarity is very close; but a general norm which comes closer to the truth is that the similarity, whether absolutely close or distant, should be relatively greater. That is, the paradigm picked should be the closest one. Thus the flying saucer was called a flying saucer not because of great and extensive similarity with a saucer but because it resembled a saucer more than it did a hammer or a shoe or even a plate. Were flying saucers familiar objects with their own familiar name, that would be the term to use (just as the term "airplane", rather than "flying machine", is now the term to use for airplanes); for between flying saucers and other flying saucers there is far greater similarity than between flying saucers and saucers. But to describe radically new or transcendent realities we must employ existing terms, with their existing uses; and then the greatest similarity may be quite distant.

Instances in which we speak of "transcendence" are often ones where the resemblance is especially distant. Impressed by the dissimilarity of referent and analogue, we perhaps assert that the words are now merely "arrows" pointing in the "direction" of the transcendent reality without really describing it. But no such switch of terminology seems called for, if this is all we have in mind. For no matter how far we stretch terms without snapping them, the same principle is operative: relative similarity, not absolute. God is more like a wise, good person than he is like a stupid, selfish one; yet doubtless the difference between him and both of them is far greater than that between the two of them. This is not all we might want to indicate by talk of "arrows" and "pointing" (we might also have in mind our ignorance of just how distant the resemblance is), but it is often the most prominent motive.

These observations may be viewed as an implicit restatement of the traditional "three ways": *via affirmativa, via negativa, via eminentiae*. In the first, much as journalists and observers spontaneously spoke of "flying saucers", so theologians and simple believers spontaneously affirm God's knowledge, love, power, presence, etc. In the second, much as we are constrained to admit that the objects sighted in the sky were not really saucers, so, reflecting on the ordinary application of terms like "know", "love", etc., we seem forced to admit that God does not really know, love, etc. In the third, much as we continue, unintimidated by ordinary usage, to speak of flying saucers, so we continue to assert God's knowledge, love, power, presence, though in an extended, higher sense. The negation results from applying the rule of absolute similarity, the final reassertion is justified by relative similarity.

4. Yet isn't this justification sheer sleight of hand? For the ex-

tension of "saucer" to the flying kind is justified by a close, though limited similarity, whereas in theology it is frequently impossible to detect any close resemblance, total or specific, to cite in behalf of an extension. Consider, for example, the familiar use of "knowledge", for true beliefs based on reasons, and contrast it with the theological use. The criteria of belief are what a person says and does; his reasons are: having looked, read in reliable sources, heard it said, proved by calculation, inferred from repeated experience, etc. And none of this applies to God. How, then, can we say that God knows? The flying saucer paradigm does not help (it may be argued), but seems rather to suggest that close similarity is indeed the rule: sometimes single and narrow, other times multiple and great.

To dissipate this impression, consider a sample from the Psalmist:

> How great are thy doings, O Lord,
> how very deep thy designs!

Such a use of "deep" or "depths" recurs frequently in the Psalter, for instance in Psalm 69:

> Save me, O God,
> for the water mounts to my chin,
> I am sunk in deep mire,
> where there is no foothold.
> I have got into deep water,
> and the flood overwhelms me.

"A poetic manner of expression," it may be said; but if so, then we are all poets, most of the time. For we speak not only of "deep wells" and "deep oceans", but of "deep meaning", "deep thought", "deep sorrow", "deep blue", "deep notes", and so on. And we stretch countless other terms in much the same fashion.

In most of these extensions, no common element can be found, nor close similarity. Where, for instance is the precise point of resemblance between a high roof and high C? In what exact respect does a sharp pain resemble a sharp knife? And is there some limited but close similarity between a deep sorrow and a deep ocean? "The impression," it is sometimes suggested, "is similar, not the thing. That is, though no property of the sea resembles our sorrow, the impression it makes on us does." But does a high roof also make the same impression on us as a high C? And when we see a sharp curve in the road, does our reaction resemble a sharp pain? And as for deep sorrow, does our feeling as we gaze into a deep pool resemble our grief at the loss of a friend? Of course not. We would never venture such hypotheses were we not inclined to think that there *must* be something common to account for the common word—if not an essence, then at least some perceptible link. But if we look instead of thinking, we often find nothing of the kind.

Nor, for that matter, do we find any overlapping in many cases we consider paradigmatic. Concerning the everyday use of a word like "blue", we might say with Wittgenstein: "Find it surprising, as you do some things which disturb you. Then the puzzling aspect of the latter will disappear, by your accepting this fact as you do the other."[6] For how does a child learn to use and understand a word like "blue"? Not by means of a definition. Nor by being shown the full spectrum of shades falling within the word's customary range. Nor by detecting a sensible sameness—"pure blue"—in the samples shown him. No, he hears this or that blue thing called blue, and proceeds to apply the same term to other shades containing no discernible element in common with the shades to which he has heard the term applied.

Notice, furthermore, that the child's extended application of "blue" is not only effective, so justified, but the best and perhaps only way he could report what he sees. No other term is available. Later, perhaps, he will learn some more precise labels, such as "turquoise" and "cobalt", or will learn about light waves and be able to indicate the shade indirectly, in scientific terms. But now he must rely on "blue". And even adults must often do likewise, because they don't know any precise term for this particular shade, or the frequency of its waves. Besides, the same situation recurs, within a narrower range, even for a term like "cobalt".

It should not surprise us, therefore, that the "extended" uses of words like "sharp", "high", "dull", "deep", are often not only effective, but irreplaceable. How else, for instance, can most of us describe certain notes than by calling them "deep"? Is this just an indirect way of stating a property we might describe directly? And do we know some alternative way of referring to "high notes"? True, this is a standard way of describing sounds, and need not have come second in the process of learning. We might have heard only notes called high or deep, and still have understood the expressions. And thereafter they might have had much the same meaning for us as for someone who first heard walls called high, or wells called deep, then extended the term himself. But often it is not so. There are cases, notes Wittgenstein, where "one might speak of a 'primary' and 'secondary' sense of a word. It is only if the word has the primary sense for you that you use it in the secondary one." For instance, "only if you have learnt to calculate—on paper or out loud—can you be made to grasp, by means of this concept, what calculating in the head is." The secondary sense, notice, "is not a 'metaphorical' sense. If I say 'For me the vowel *e* is yellow' I do not mean: 'yellow' in a metaphorical sense—for I could not express what I want to say in any other way than by means of the idea 'yellow'."[7]

"Now, I say nothing about the causes of this phenomenon. They *might* be associations from my childhood. But that is a hypothesis. Whatever the explanation—the inclination is there."[8] For no evident *reason*, "a *concept* forces itself on one."[9] It would go against the grain, for example, to call our sorrow "high" or high C "low". Yet we detect no basis of comparison between the grief and other things we call deep, or between high C and other things we call high. These predications are not motivated in the way "flying saucer" was.

5. Let us cast a quick glance back over the preceding samples. Between car and car the resemblances are multiple. Between saucer and flying saucer there is at least one. But between the depths of which the Psalmist spoke and those of the Atlantic, no link appears. And countless such extensions occur. For instance, "Let us ask the question 'What is the similarity between looking for a word in your memory and looking for my friend in the park?' What would be the answer to such a question? . . . One might be inclined to say, 'Surely a similarity must strike us, or we shouldn't be moved to use the same word.'—Compare that statement with this: 'A similarity between these cases must strike us in order that we should be inclined to use the same picture to represent both.' This says that some act must precede the act of using this picture. But why shouldn't what we call 'the similarity striking us' consist partially or wholly in our using the same picture? And why shouldn't it consist partially or wholly in our being prompted to use the same phrase?"[10]

These remarks of Wittgenstein suggest how mistaken it would be to take the principle of relative similarity as a new, albeit looser, rule replacing the strict one of absolute similarity. It was offered as a corrective to that norm, not as a substitute straitjacket. For a flying saucer may be more like a saucer than like a plate, and God's provident love may resemble a father's love more than it does a child's, but does the letter *e resemble* a yellow object, or a dull pain *resemble* a dull knife, or a deep blue *resemble* a deep well? And even if we do choose to stretch the terms "resemble" and "similar" that far, so as to cover all cases, it is clear that the rule of relative similarity would then be no rule at all. It would draw no limit, provide no guidance.

Furthermore, it would be misleading. In many an instance, like that of the flying saucers, it seems apt enough to say (as I did some pages back): "The similarity, whether absolutely close or distant, should be relatively greater. That is, the paradigm picked should be the closest one." However, in other cases a more distant paradigm may be not only licit, but preferable. As an illustration of my meaning, and of the danger of absolute norms, consider this further sample:

> "Do you think Sanchez will crack under the pressure? They have some pretty effective ways to make people talk, you know." "No, Sanchez is a rock. They'll never break him."

The word "rock" (or "crack", or "break"), it would often be said, is here applied in an "improper" or "figurative" sense. It is a mere metaphor. True, the figurative expression may be more forceful and colorful, so can be tolerated in ordinary conversation and still more readily in poetry; but for sober-headed description of fact, more straightforward terms are of course preferable. They describe reality more accurately. However, if we consider the actual functioning of the sentence, "Sanchez is a rock," we see that it leaves nothing to be desired. In fact it may be apter, not only rhetorically, but also descriptively, than a good many "proper" predications we might think of. For, thanks to the context, its meaning is quite precise.

An example of "proper" predication would be the use of the word "car" for any of the specimens previously mentioned. If a person says he saw a funny car in the circus, his hearer may not know what to expect. If he says he bought a car, but is a certain type of college student, again his hearer should be ready for anything. And even if an ordinary person tells us that he has just bought a car, if we know nothing about his finances, tastes, or reasons for buying, the possibilities range from Rolls Royce to beach buggy. But now consider the description of Sanchez. He is not a rock the way a hunk of granite is, nor even the way an apostle is, or a guard for the Chicago Bears. No, the hearer in our sample dialog knows just what sort of firmness is meant: Sanchez can stand up under torture. He knows it as surely as though that longer, more prosaic form of expression had been used: "Sanchez can stand up under torture." And before claiming that this is a preferable mode of speech, at least for descriptive purposes, we might ask ourselves whether it would be better for the child to report: "I saw something whose color resembled that of the thing you called blue last week." No, the one word "blue" does the job best, and so does the one word "rock".

If we do not attend to the workings of words, we may easily succumb to an illusion like this: "To call Sanchez a rock is to say that he resembles a rock. To call a beach buggy a car is to say it resembles other cars. But it resembles other cars far more than he does a rock. So the one is an approximate, imperfect description, whereas the other is accurate." As a further refinement on this analysis, one perhaps picks out that particular aspect of a rock's makeup which serves as basis for the comparison, and points out that even between this precise trait and the firmness of Sanchez the analogy is quite distant. There is greater similarity between a beach buggy and a Rolls Royce than there is between the hardness of a rock and the firmness of a human being.

In actual discourse, however, no one who heard a person called a rock would suppose for a moment that he possessed the physical properties of granite. The cognitive content actually conveyed, if analytically unpacked and put in words, would not mention rocks. Nor, in the setting I have described, would it mention the rock-like solidity of a lineman or the staunch fidelity of an apostle, even in disjunctive form. The hearer might believe these things, too, of Sanchez, but not in virtue of the statement. That conveys or confirms belief in just the sort of mental toughness required to endure torture. The informative content, therefore, may be *sharper* than for "I bought a car."

In theology, a similar illusion might take this cognate form: "To say that God is a father is to say he resembles a certain kind of human being. To say he is a rock is to say he resembles, say, a hunk of granite. But the resemblance between God and man is greater than the resemblance between God and rock. So the former predication is more perfect than the latter, though of course both are very imperfect. The best we can do in theology is to predicate attributes which imply no imperfection, as does the term 'father'. Thus if we say of God that he is a being, we must make allowance for the analogy of being, but the statement is more accurate than when we call God a father, and far more accurate than when we call him a rock. That is a mere metaphor."

The idea is that there are levels of predication which correspond to grades of being. The rock is at the bottom, then comes man, and far above is the divine nature. Thus a term for the rock is least appropriate in theology, a term for man comes closer, and a term applied quite generally to angels, God, and man is the highest and best of all. Therefore, if we would speak about the constancy of God, "rock" is the least apt description, "steadfast" is somewhat better, and "unchanging" is better than either.

To see where the error lies this time, let us consider the first contrast, between "rock" and "steadfast". The supposed advantage of the latter lies in its being applied (despite its origin) just to people and not to rocks. But the pragmatic consequence of this difference is that "rock" is, if anything, a better term than "steadfast" with which to describe God. For human character is not like granite, but notoriously chalk-like and crumbly. To call a man a rock is to say that he is *exceptionally* strong and steadfast. The figure is hyperbolic. And since a typical scriptural or liturgical setting in which we call God a rock indicates a moral sense as clearly as in our sample, the term "rock", being hyperbolic, comes *closer* to the divine reality than does a more human term, suggesting mere human steadfastness.

It is necessary, therefore, to divest expressions such as "figurative", "proper", "improper", "mere metaphor" of value content. They usually indicate neither virtues nor defects, but such facts as majority use, priority in time, causal dependence. Since a theologian is generally interested instead in effectiveness of communication and accuracy of content, and since these traditional expressions have so often been thought to indicate differences of this order, I would suggest that the reader banish them from his mind for the duration of this chapter, and of the book. Otherwise he may unwittingly relegate to the dustbin the very expressions which are most illuminating for the study of theological sayings.

Terms like "figurative" and "improper" are dangerous in this way too: they may suggest simplistic dichotomies where there is in fact a continuum of cases. Consider, for instance, the various applications of a word like "tight": "tight shoe", "tight knot", "tight rope", "tight curve", "tight squeeze", "tight money", "tight fist", "tight ship", "tight control", and so on. Which of these are "proper", "literal" uses of the term, which "figurative"? Or reflect on the example just considered, and on the following series of expressions: if we say that God is unchanging—constant—faithful—steadfast—firm—rock-like— a rock, where does the "proper" end and the "improper" begin? What is "mere metaphor", what not? No answer comes. Yet this is but one meager series in the sea of symbolism, where the shadings and variations are innumerable. As we continue along the continuum, therefore, from meaningful to meaningless, it will be well to empty our minds of familiar terminology based on irrelevant considerations, and to examine instead the actual operation of the terms, within the given context.

6.   A water diviner has been called in, to help locate a well site. After wandering around for a while, he suddenly declares, "I feel water twenty feet down."

Why did even the later Wittgenstein (at least in 1933) have misgivings about such a statement as this and feel that the diviner owes us an explanation of his meaning?[11] Can't we think of various possibilities the words might express, and doesn't our inability to say which one is meant conform to the general elasticity of language noted in the first two samples? "The book is on the table" means: "It is on the far edge *or* on the near edge *or* in the middle *or*. . . ." Likewise, we might argue, "I feel water twenty feet down" means: "I have a feeling which has been associated in my experience with the presence of water twenty feet under the ground; or, I have a feeling which I have found to be associated with water near the surface and whose intensity is proportional to the water's nearness; or . . ." True, the water diviner employs an unusual way of speaking, but isn't the cognitive effect basically similar?

Perhaps. But consider, for instance, the expression "feeling blue". Imagine that someone heard this expression for the first time. Could he legitimately conclude: "He has a feeling which is associated with his seeing something blue or which excites images of blue objects or which. . . ."? Or suppose someone heard the expression "see red" for the first time. Would he be justified in concluding that the person had *seen* something? The meanings of words, said Wittgenstein, are not like atmospheres which they carry with them into every context and every combination. A radically different context or verbal combination may bring a radical shift of meaning. Guessing is then too wide-open to do any good. Unless we are familiar with that sort of combination in that sort of setting, cognitive communication may be nil. An expression which can mean anything is in the same category as a Chinese word slipped into an unrevealing English sequence; it has no meaning for us. We don't understand it.

This argument too requires closer scrutiny. It sounds very logical; a person "should not" conclude so readily that the diviner has had a feeling which is somehow associated with water under the ground. But he probably would. I did; the business about "feeling blue" was an afterthought. And if in fact the diviner was talking about a feeling, then nothing has gone wrong. Language is simply functioning as it usually functions, with disregard for abstract logical ideals. There is no mechanism at the heart of language or thought determining the ways in which words *must* be taken. People simply do react to words in one way or another, and their basic affinity with the speaker, both in nature and in upbringing, makes for satisfactory communication in the majority of cases. If the diviner's similarity to the rest of us results in his speaking of a feeling and in our supposing a feeling, then skeptical demands for "justification" are out of place. They are irrelevant to cognitive analysis. This point, too, is important for the realistic analysis of theological statements. The formulae by which revelation is conveyed do not need to satisfy the "ideal" criteria of logicians but to achieve communication with the mass of mankind. And the analyst's job is to see what does happen, not to decide *a priori* what should happen.

If we do not feel misgivings about extensions like "sharp pain" and "deep sorrow" but do about the diviner's innovative saying, doubtless one reason is that we are familiar with the former and know that they work. Furthermore, we can sense why they do: shared experience, in addition to common nature, makes the extension natural. We too have felt deep sorrow, sharp pain, high hopes, heavy foreboding; and we generally see other people depressed or ugly before we hear such phrases as "feel blue" or "black mood". The diviner, however, though he may be basically similar to the rest of us, seems to have experiences which we do not. So it appears less likely that in this case we would "catch on".

Yet there are degrees of "catching on". If we supposed that he had felt something and he did, that would be one degree of communication. If we judged what sort of feeling it was, that would be another degree. It is this latter precision of understanding which the lack of shared experience causes to appear unlikely. But before deciding that the exchange is thereby rendered null and void, we should remember that neither did Jim know *where* on the table the math book lay. And if his mother had replied, "It's in the dining room," he would not have known it was on the table. And on another occasion the answer might have been, "You left it home." Or even, "You left it in the States." Compared with such statements as this last, the diviner's saying seems respectable enough, even if his hearers have never felt just the way he did. Who has been everywhere in the United States?

"But we might at least go there." Yes, and it is conceivable that we should one day have the same experience the diviner did, and exclaim, "Aha, so that's what he meant! Now I know what he was talking about!" That would be our natural verbal reaction, but it should not lead us to suppose that previously we had *no* idea what he was talking about, no inkling of his meaning. Rather it would be like going into the living room, seeing the book on the table, and thereby acquiring more precise information about the book's location than the words "It's on the living room table" conveyed. Jim's mother, like the diviner, may have possessed quite precise knowledge, but her words, though perfectly accurate, were not precise; their meaning did not match the precision of her knowledge. Neither did the diviner's.

It is of course characteristic of truly informative utterances that prior to their occurrence the speaker knows more than the hearer. But it is no similar tautology to say that the speaker often, perhaps generally, knows more about the matter of discourse than his words express. In the case of the diviner, though, we have gone farther and supposed not only that he has fuller, more precise knowledge than his hearer, both before and after his utterance, but that his hearer is in no position to acquire this supplementary refinement of knowledge. He has not had that sort of experience and perhaps never will. In a stronger than ordinary sense, therefore, the truth communicated to him "transcends his experience". In the following example, this transcendence, though perhaps not greater, is more evident.

7.   When Ted acquired his scarlet hot-rod, both family and friends joshed him about it. "Why?" asked Bill, his blind

brother. "What's so funny about scarlet?" "Well," they said, "it's as though
he were to go about blowing a trumpet
wherever he went." "Is scarlet like a
trumpet note, then?" "Well, insofar as
a color can be, yes, it is."

The present example differs from the preceding one in several respects. For one thing, discussion of the water diviner's
words is rendered vague and hypothetical by the fact that we
too, like the ones hearing the statement, have no clear idea
what, if anything, he would have felt, and what relation his
feeling would have had to water in the ground. Scarlet and
trumpet notes, however, are familiar and unmysterious. We
know what experience the others have had and Bill has not,
and we know what degree of similarity there is between that
experience and the sound of a trumpet. Furthermore, we can
sense just how far words have now been stretched, farther
probably than we imagined in the case of the diviner.

It is instructive to note that we could plausibly and naturally
go through the whole *via positiva* and *via negativa* of traditional theodicy with regard to this example too, and would end
up with fewer qualms than we do when the alternation of affirmation and negation is highly abstract and we are thus apparently left with nothing but a set of contrasting, perhaps contradictory expressions. If, for instance, we start with the
assertion that God is wise, then proceed to deny that he is wise
in any of the ways human beings are wise, we may seem to
have taken away with one hand what we gave with the other.
The end result, it may appear, is nothing but the word "wise",
voided of all content. Such *may* sometimes be the result, but
the present example shows that it need not be. Of scarlet we
might reasonably say that it is not at all like a trumpet note.
We might insist that a color is not a sound, that one is visual
and the other auditory, one inseparable from extension and the
other not, one an extended property and the other temporal,

one constitutive of objects and the other not, and so on. It is plain nonsense, we might declare, to stretch terms so. No doctrine of natural theology could be made to look sillier. Yet the plain fact is: the comparison was excellently chosen. It is difficult to think of anything better that might have been said to the blind man. He now has a fair idea of why Ted is joshed. Tooling through town in a scarlet hot-rod is not like walking down the street in one's shorts, nor is it laughable the way a false nose would be. Nor is it as though Ted drove facing the rear, or had stripped his car to the chassis and let his passengers ride in a bath tub. No, it is more as though the horn on his car were a trumpet and he missed no chance to toot it.

Furthermore, were Bill to receive his sight, say through an operation, he could probably pick out his brother's car from dingier ones on the block. The color would hit him as it hits us, as "brilliant", "loud", "striking"—like a trumpet note—and he would then josh along with the rest. I am not suggesting, notice, that having heard these terms applied both to familiar things like trumpet notes and to unfamiliar scarlet, he would now detect a common essence in the color he sees, or even a family resemblance with the other referents, and thereby conclude that the color must be scarlet. My point is rather that he too, being a typical human being, would react in the way which accounts for our calling both scarlet and trumpet notes "brilliant", "loud", "striking", etc. He would sense an affinity where we do. Or put it this way: if an ordinary human being finds the comparison with a trumpet note more natural than a comparison with a flute or violin, and if on the other hand he would not compare brown, green, black, gray or mauve with a trumpet note, then Bill, when he became completely normal through the gift of sight and was faced with a choice between brown, green, black, gray, mauve, and scarlet cars, might be expected to pick scarlet as the color they had compared with a trumpet note. Or if that didn't work, he might at least consider scarlet the color they would most likely joke about. And if none of these connections was any help, then Bill simply would not be the typical human being I meant him to be.

In the supposition, then, that the comparison with a trumpet note, in its overall context, did permit him to make the right choice, his act of picking out the car, though long delayed, would be comparable to Jim's act when he went to the living room and looked on the table. A statement can have cognitive content even if acted on much later, in fact even if it is never acted on. For knowledge, as was previously remarked, is a disposition, not an act. Jim's knowing the book's position is not equivalent to his getting it. His mother may fetch it instead.

8. Suppose, though, that the blind man never receives his sight. Isn't this the situation with regard to many religious truths? Don't we pass our lives without being able to do anything with them? Doesn't their content remain as inaccessible as colors to a man blind at birth and blind till the day he dies? And in that case are the doctrines really informative? What good does it do us to know that a revealed doctrine is backed by the pure gold of analogy if we can never draw on any of the gold, if it remains locked in celestial vaults? Can a doctrine even be true if it conveys no information?

These vague misgivings may be more precisely stated in terms of cognitive pattern. We started, remember, with loose disjunctions (edge, middle, etc.; salmon, carmine, etc.), each of whose members was known to the hearer; then passed to a looser, more complex disjunction (sport cars, convertibles, etc.), in which most of the members were still common knowledge; then advanced to a case in which it was dubious whether the referent (the diviner's feeling) was one which the hearers had come across or could become acquainted with; and finally to a case where the hearer (the blind man) clearly had not and could not make himself acquainted with the referent. This referent, notice, did not merely lie beyond the range of his experience, actual or possible. No, he knew it did. So for him there was no disjunctive content. Tell a man who has never seen scarlet that your scarlet car is red and he may suppose that it is rose or carmine or magenta or some other shade he is familiar with. The statement has plenty of experiential content. But tell a man blind from birth that scarlet is like a trumpet note and he knows perfectly well that you do not mean it is an electric shock or the clash of cymbals or any other thing with which he is familiar and with which he may feel inclined to compare a trumpet note. He knows he is in the dark. With this illustration in mind, therefore, we may restate the difficulty and ask: If neither the past nor the subsequent experience of a hearer (at least in this life) provides any disjunctive content for a statement—if neither then nor afterwards can he suggest or encounter any instance whatsoever of the sort of thing described—is the statement really informative? And what if *all* hearers are in this situation? The following sample was chosen for the light it may throw on this issue.

> "I have it!", exclaims Professor M. "I've found a method for controlling nuclear fusion!" A meeting is hurriedly called to hear the explanation, but on his way to it Professor M is killed in a traffic accident. The search continues, in vain, for years; no way is found to harness nuclear fusion.

Here is a case where no specimen method nor disjunction of possible methods forms the content of the statement. No such information is conveyed to any hearer. No one but the speaker can suggest a single specific way in which fusion might be controlled. True, scientists might suggest solutions "by means of a vacuum", "by means of lasers", "by means of a magnetic field", and so on. But the problem would remain: they could give no specific content for these general descriptions; they could suggest no sample instances. Yet we would hesitate to declare the professor's statement meaningless or uninformative on this account. We would not immediately reinterpret his words as, for instance, a veiled exhortation to search harder. Yet this is true: the only way his declaration affected our lives might be to make us search harder, with greater hope of success and with greater confidence in the very intelligibility of the goal. If we believed his statement, we would not fear a hidden contradiction in the proposal.

This analysis suggests how to assess the reinterpretations that are frequently offered of doctrinal statements, translating them into moral, pragmatic terms. Consider, for instance, the reinterpretation of "God is good" as an exhortation to charity or as the statement of an ethical ideal. It is true, first of all, that such a teaching may have the same effect as an exhortation to charity. It is also true that the statement may have that as its aim, even its principal aim. Furthermore, just such pragmatic consequences are the basis for our saying that someone knows something; that is, the actions a person performs are an important criterion of knowledge, so determine the cognitive content of a statement. To judge the informative power of an utterance we must consider its influence on the actions of typical hearers (for instance, where Jim looks for the book, what car Bill picks out, and so on). But this is true of all statements, and it does not turn them all into commands or exhortations. Pragmatic reinterpretations tend to overlook the possibility that an utterance not only has the outer form of a statement of fact but is backed by ontological analogy; and that the speaker is aware of this objective backing and has it in mind when he makes the statement; and that he intends to be understood in this sense, as playing the language-game of informative discourse; and that the truth of his words may be brought home to his hearers, either here or hereafter, in ways they do not now suspect. What makes facile reinterpretations so natural is the amount of truth they contain. What makes them so unfortunate is the likelihood that by turning revealed truths into exhortations such as any preacher can mass-produce, they may void revelation of its unique power to affect our lives, through its status as revealed and transcendent truth. Think how little effect the professor's words would have on research if they were regarded as mere encouragement to look harder.

"Still, do we learn anything from his statement?" Yes, we do. If we take his word for it and he is right, we learn that he performed an action which can properly be called finding, and that what he discovered can properly be called a method, for what can appropriately be termed harnessing nuclear fusion. If it be objected that this information is merely linguistic, since we can envisage neither the finding nor the method nor the harnessing, the answer is that linguistic information, too, is information. If a bridge stretches off into impenetrable mist, and someone who has traversed it assures you that it touches a farther bank, this too is information, even though the bank is invisible and its distance unknown. The same analysis, notice, and the same comparison apply to any transcendent revelation with which theologians are concerned. In each instance we acquire at least this linguistic kind of information. And of course to call it linguistic does not mean it concerns only words. Language extends as far as reality.

9. None of the preceding samples stretches language to the breaking point. But what of this one:

> "Do you have many friends in the department, professor?" "Why yes," he replied straightfaced; "take the cube root of 383 and you'll find the precise number." His questioner, not being up on cube roots, answered a little uncertainly that it sounded like a considerable number.

Though this may be one hearer's reaction, it is no sure indication of the statement's content. For a "considerable number" of friends would be eight or nine or ten, etc., and none of these numbers satisfies the professor's formula. None of them is the cube root of 383. To a certain extent, therefore, this statement resembles the previous sample; there too no one could suggest a verifying instance. However, this professor's statement does not send his hearers off in search of the missing root. For anyone with a smattering of math knows an appropriate root can't be found. And the difficulty here lies not with the limited intelligence of man but in the statement. It does not make sense.

The reason for saying so seems clear enough. We can work out this problem and see that the answer is not an integer. And it does not make sense to say that a person has 7.3 friends. However, this verdict on the professor's facetious reply is not evident to anyone who lacks the necessary mathematical training or who doesn't trouble to work out the answer. Thus the sample serves as paradigm for the numerous theological and philosophical utterances which employ meaningful expressions and correct grammar to make statements which are apparently meaningful, but which, upon analysis, turn out to be irredeemably incoherent and void of sense. Since neither their sense nor their lack of sense is evident, they may be considered profound, much as the professor's non-mathematical hearer received his words with respect and even supposed that he grasped their general drift.

What is not typical is the ease and certainty with which we arrive at the verdict. To at least a good many people it is clear that the professor's statement makes no sense. And those who know no mathematics, realizing their limitations, are not likely to contest the verdict. In this respect the scientist's claim, in #8, resembles problematic theological statements more closely. Upon closer examination of the problem, some physicist might claim that the proposal of controlling nuclear fusion involves an impossibility comparable to that formulated by Heisenberg in the Uncertainty Principle. Others might disagree, as some did with Heisenberg; for the problem is complex. Thus no sharp, evident border separates sense from nonsense. Another important way in which the borderline is blurred emerges from the following example.

10.   Many people have searched for a way to trisect the angle with just ruler and compass; or at least that is what they said they were trying to do. And some people have claimed to have found a method. It has, however, been demonstrated that the proposal states a logical impossibility; there is no possible way of trisecting the angle with just ruler and compass.

In the circumstances, how should we judge a person's claim that he has solved the problem? Does his statement, "I have found a way to trisect the angle" make any more sense than the statement "I have 7.3 friends"? Here, as in #9 but not in #8, neither speaker nor hearer can provide an illustrative instance of the thing described, and the possibility of instantiation is ruled out *a priori*. Though with much greater difficulty than in #9, the proposal is revealed to be logically incoherent. So if we called example #9 nonsense, shouldn't we say the same of #10? Shouldn't we call the statement nonsense?

According to some ideal of abstract logic, maybe so. But suppose somebody did say to you, "I've found a way to trisect the angle." Would you reply, "What you say doesn't make sense," or, "You are talking nonsense"? Wouldn't you say, "I'm afraid you are mistaken; it has been shown to be impossible to trisect the angle"? And yet you would say the professor of #9 was talking nonsense if he said he had 7.3 friends. Why is that? One natural response would be, "I know what it would be like to trisect an angle, but I have no idea what it would be like to have 7.3 friends." But what would it be like to trisect an angle using just ruler and compass? Granted, it would be something like bisecting an angle with ruler and compass, if any comparison were possible. But similarly, having 7.3 friends would doubtless resemble having 7 friends, if there were two such situations to compare. The mystery remains.

What then is the problem? It is the difficulty of finding a clear, consistent norm which determines our use of terms like "sense" and "nonsense", "meaningful" and "meaningless". But isn't that what we should expect? Conceptual borderlines are normally fuzzy and fluctuating, even when the concept is as simple as "book" or "car". What wonder then that no clear, consistent criterion has been established in common usage for the application of semantic terms. Common usage, after all, consists of the practice not only of savants but of housewives, businessmen, and paper boys. And even savants know precious little about the functioning of language. It is not conceivable that such a populace should distinguish sharply and consistently between cases like those here considered. Accordingly, faced with these rather unusual samples and the still stranger analyses, we react now one way and now another, without any clear direction from the words' use in the language (that is, the use of "sense", "nonsense", etc.), and without any clear apprehension of what influences determine our reactions. One time we think, perhaps, of all the people who have actually tried to trisect the angle, so judge a claim of success to be meaningful. Another time the conceptual incoherence may seem more obvious (e.g., 7.3 friends), so we judge the statement meaningless. But no one consideration consistently governs such semantic discriminations.

11. True, fairly evident incoherence we tend to call nonsense, well-concealed incoherence not. But this does not show that obviousness is the criterion we follow in applying the predicate "meaningless". It seems more reasonable to suggest that incoherence is our norm, but that to apply it we need to see the incoherence (as we need to see the incongruity to find a joke funny). And since the mere assertion by experts that the angle cannot be trisected provides no view of the proposal's ultimate incoherence, we continue to call it meaningful. However, dif-

ficulties arise for either criterion from a sample like the following, where the incoherence is as evident as for 7.3 friends, yet the verdict doubtless differs:

> A politician, thundering against the opposition, declared that their policies had "opened the flood gates to a general conflagration".

We laugh at this, as also at the slip of a well-known pulpit orator, who lamented something or other which had "erected a chasm between us". But we have no difficulty with the general meaning of either declaration, despite the amusing phantasms that may float through our minds, of a fire flooding the land or of a chasm being hoisted into place. Taken strictly, the words "erect a chasm" or "open flood gates to a conflagration" are as nonsensical as the expression "7.3 friends". But in such circumstances we don't take the words strictly. Their cognitive effect on the hearer hardly differs from that of a better-turned phrase.

I shall not attend to the possible causes of this difference, but shall just note the fact: though the verbal incoherence is similar, the result is not. One statement we understand, the other we don't. One we could readily translate into coherent expressions—"calamitous", "divisive"—the other not. So one we would probably term meaningful, the other not. Thus the politician's statement fits as follows into our continuum of cases: (a) it resembles #9 (fractional friends) and differs from #10 (trisecting the angle) in its more obvious incoherence; (b) on the other hand, it resembles #10 (trisection) and differs from #9 (friends) in being less readily labeled meaningless; (c) but it differs from both #9 and #10 in conveying a readily intelligible message, which might be expressed in apter terms.

This final trait serves as a warning: we had better be careful, when dealing with theological statements, that we do not judge too facilely from mere surface symptoms of logical incoherence. Language can play us endless tricks; it can veil good sense as well as nonsense. Occasion will arise to remember this lesson in the discussion of *Casti Connubii* in Chapter Five.

12. An Omaha woman, asked by an interviewer about her television habits, replied, "Oh, I never watch television. I turn it off more than I turn it on." As it stands, this sample belongs with the sayings just quoted, of the preacher and the politician: same surface incoherence, same ready understanding, same easy translation into coherent terms. But suppose, now, that we expand the dialog as follows:

> "Ma'm, could you tell me about your television habits?" "Oh, I turn it off more than I turn it on." "You mean other members of the family turn it on and you then turn it off?" "Certainly not; that would be rude." "Sorry. Do you mean, then, that you seldom watch television?" "Well, I wouldn't say that. It's frequently on, but I take little interest." "I see. Other members of the family are more interested than you, and they turn it on." "Oh, I don't think our family takes more interest in television than most." Sensing defeat, the interviewer thanks his host and departs.

Now what interpretation should we give to the words "I turn it off more than I turn it on"? And how should we classify them: meaningful? meaningless? Consider the facts: (a) on the one hand, no evident sense emerges here as it did in the preceding sample; (b) on the other hand, neither is any calculation possible which reveals unmistakable incoherence, as in the case of trisection or the professor's friends. Having found the cube of 383, we reach a clear conclusion. Having proved the impossibility of the trisection, we rule it out once for all. But here no such step seems possible. So we cannot say simply, definitively,

"That's nonsense," as we can for fractional friends. But neither, on the other hand, can we say that the statement makes sense. For, *what* sense?

We might ask the same question about an ambiguous assertion. And noting the impossibility of specifying *a* sense, we might hesitate to acknowledge that the assertion has any sense. But in the present case the difficulty extends farther. For an ordinary ambiguous utterance leaves two or three possibilities open, whereas in an exchange like the preceding, each alternative seems to be cancelled in turn. Thus at the start the interviewer might think that the puzzling statement meant merely that the lady seldom watched television. But that meaning she later denied, or seemed to deny, or rejected as an explanation of her words. On the other hand, she also denied turning off the programs that others turned on, and gave no hint that her puzzling statement should be taken literally as a statistical summary. The closest thing to an explanation was her admission of disinterest; but that remark, though intelligible, could hardly provide a meaning for the words "I turn it off more than I turn it on." So if we are left empty-handed in this case, it is for a very different reason than in a typical instance of ambiguity. There each alternative fits the words, and none is ruled out. Here each seems ruled out, either by the troublesome words themselves or by others in the dialog. Thus, in its simple way, the exchange resembles many a speculative discourse, including some we shall consider.

13. Modify the preceding sample, and it still differs from typical cases of ambiguity, but differently:

> The interviewer meets the same lady coming out the front door. "I turn it off more than I turn it on," she declares, distraught. "Pardon, Ma'm, but what do you turn off more than you turn it on?" "Why, the other one," she replies, and continues on her way.

The cognitive blackout in a case like this results not from the canceling of possibilities, as in the previous sample, nor from the survival of several clear alternatives, as in a case of ambiguity, but from poverty of context and explanation. The possibilities are left wide open. This, too, despite the oddity of the example, is a common pattern.

If we hesitate, nonetheless, to call the statement meaningless, doubtless that is because we can think of many things the lady could be referring to, and feel sure that she had one of them in mind and could easily indicate what it was. So the illustration is not perfect for my purposes. It does illustrate the difference between many speculative assertions and cases of mere ambiguity. But it does not illustrate adequately the more total obscurity sometimes encountered in theoretical discussions: the difficulty of conceiving any plausible interpretation, the suspicion that the author himself could not enlighten us.

Such statements as these, and others like the previous one, in the fruitless interview, I shall also call meaningless, along with more evident nonsense like the bit about fractional friends. That is, I shall extend the term "meaningless" to assertions for which no intelligible content can be found, either because the clues are too few or because, though plentiful, they conflict. This may be a departure from usage; but if so, it is a slight one. No shift of borders is involved. I am merely sharpening somewhat a vague and flexible boundary. These sample utterances some might call meaningless, others not. I shall. For I would like to use the handy terms "meaningful" and "meaningless", to say something definite enough to have some significance. And the type of vacuity just illustrated has notable significance. Asked to believe such declarations, we would not know what to believe. Asked to trace the belief in Scripture or tradition, we would not know what to look for. Asked to argue for or against, we could not even begin. Such, in what follows, will be the import of the label "meaningless".

It is important that this terminology and the reason for it be kept in mind. Otherwise the reader may receive my verdicts, particularly the negative ones, with skepticism. They will seem arbitrary, facile, unfair. For going just by the ordinary fluid use of terms like "meaningful" and "meaningless", one might well hesitate in such cases. When I hesitate less, I shall not be dogmatizing. Nor shall I be assuming sharper insight into the concepts "meaningful" and "meaningless", or access to hidden facts unknown to the reader. In keeping with the terminology just proposed, it will suffice for me to establish similarity with the preceding cases: similar vacuity, similar incoherence. For that is what I shall mean by the designation "meaningless". The very samples labeled will provide further illustration of the suggested sense.

The methodological implications of this terminology should also be noted. For, reading remarks about lack of sense, a person would naturally think of a clear example, such as "I have $\sqrt[3]{383}$ friends," rather than of nebulous, complex samples like those just cited. And the incoherence of that proposition can be demonstrated decisively, by simply calculating the root, whereas no such conclusive demonstration is conceivable for the further paradigms I have chosen to term meaningless. What would it mean, for instance, to "prove" that the lady's remark in #12 is meaningless? At most, that we have tried all likely interpretations and have found none that works. But how could we prove that we have tested all likely interpretations? Mightn't one have been overlooked? To this challenge we can only reply, "Which one?" And such an answer will fail to satisfy anyone who has the clearer paradigm in mind, and derives from it his notion of an acceptable demonstration. Hence the necessity of noting the further samples I have listed as meaningless. For it is not to be expected that dubious philosophical or theological doctrines can generally be shown to be incoherent through a mere calculation, evident to all. Such theories typically resemble "I turn it off more than I turn it on" more than they do "I have $\sqrt[3]{383}$ friends." And they must be treated accordingly.

CHAPTER THREE

Moral Meaning

"**F**aith and morals" is the traditional expression Vatican I used to define the area within which infallibility is operative. The complex dichotomy thus alluded to accounts for the pairing of this chapter with the last. There I treated factual statements, about cars and tables and friends; here I must consider moral discourse, and appropriate samples. For not only is ethical teaching a major component of Christian revelation, but it is a particularly crucial and problematic one today, raising especially thorny questions with respect to meaning.

My aim, as in the last chapter, will be to lay groundwork for the later discussion of complex cases, in Chapters Four and Five. First with respect to an ethical thesis, in Chapter Four, then with respect to a magisterial statement on morals, in Chapter Five, I shall ask the basic question: Is it meaningful? As preparation, I must first consider what a meaningful moral statement looks like, so as not to judge by inappropriate standards or apply mistaken models.

It has been suggested of late that moral statements resemble ejaculations, commands, prohibitions, or performative utterances more than they do informative assertions. Quite generally, their meaning is, for instance, emotive, not factual. Thus another broad challenge is posed, analogous to that discussed in Chapter One, and calling perhaps for a similar solution. Faced there by the choice between the blanket acceptance of theological and metaphysical statements as meaningful and their blanket rejection by logical positivists, I suggested that the truth lay in between, and that though it was surely nonsense to call all such propositions meaningless, there were just as surely some that would not pass muster if examined attentively. Now a similar compromise might seem called for here: some moral statements are certainly cognitive and informative, but doubtless some slip by under false pretenses; we must just look closely to see which is which. However, for reasons which I shall indicate, I do not think that this is the appropriate answer. There is a parallel between the two cases, but it does not work out this way.

To reach a fairly accurate, comprehensive view of moral statements, it will be helpful to examine first the thesis that the⁄ are instructive, then the antithesis that they are emotive, and finally see what truth there is in each position, so as to reach a synthetic solution. The terrain is too vast and the problems are too numerous and complex for me to attempt more than a bird's-eye view, but for the same reason that is probably the most helpful thing I could achieve. Above all, people need a model of moral reasoning and discourse which is both perspicuous and valid. Such may be the result of the dialectical procedure, and the process itself serves to group much material in a logical, structured fashion, reflecting the actual course of recent debate.

First, the thesis position. Given the surface similarities between ethical statements and others, whose functioning is less complex and is clearly descriptive, it is natural that most people, including philosophers, should have assumed that moral statements, too, are descriptive. That is, the verbal parallel between "My car is red" or "She heard a loud crash," on the one hand, and "Murder is wrong" or "He did the right thing", on the other hand, may suggest that these statements function in basically similar fashion, the first stating physical properties, the second moral properties. As the redness of an object is perceptible by sight, so moral goodness is intuitable by the moral sense of man. The process by which we reach moral judgments may be longer and more complex, but none of that complexity enters the content of the judgment. To grasp the basic affinity, in this respect, between moral and non-moral statements, imagine that I assert "His car is red" not on the basis of personal observation, but because he told me so, or because that make of car is always red, or because I know his color preferences, or because he is fire chief, or because I've seen a color photo of his car. No one will then say that my statement refers to these reasons, or that the redness of the car is identical with the make of the car, the redness of the photo, the words he spoke, his color preferences, or his job as fire chief. It would be a similar error, an ethical realist might argue, to identify the goodness or badness of an action with the circumstances or consequences cited for or against it. When we say an action is right or wrong, we do not state our grounds, but indicate a distinct property, as objective as the grounds but of a different order.

To this descriptive thesis the emotive theory of A.J. Ayer in *Language, Truth, and Logic* opposes a categorical antithesis[1]:

Sentences which simply express moral judgments do not say anything. They are pure expressions of feeling and as such do not come under the category of truth and falsehood. They are unverifiable for the same reason as a cry of pain or a word of command is unverifiable—because they do not express genuine propositions.[2]

The presence of an ethical symbol in a proposition adds nothing to its factual content. Thus if I say to someone, "You acted wrongly in stealing that money," I am not stating anything more than if I had simply said, "You stole that money." In adding that this action is wrong I am not making any further statement about it. I am simply evincing my moral disapproval of it. It is as if I had said, "You stole that money," in a peculiar tone of horror, or written it with the addition of some special exclamation marks. The tone, or the exclamation marks, adds nothing to the literal meaning of the sentence. It merely serves to show that the expression of it is attended by certain feelings in the speaker.[3]

It is characteristic of the opposed poles in such philosophical confrontations that both thesis and antithesis share some basic error, which accounts for their coexistence, so that when this error is removed the polarity disappears and the synthetic truth appears. In the present instance, I think that two basic shortcomings need to be noted: first, an unreflective, simplistic view of language, and second, an equally unreflective, simplistic conception of philosophical method. The former defect has been considerably diminished of late by the influence, above all, of Wittgenstein. The latter—more profound and therefore less readily noted—has been less affected by his criticism. Let us consider each in turn.

Ayer's remark that a moral statement "p is wrong" is equivalent to "p!", where the exclamation mark "merely serves to show that the expression . . . is attended by certain feelings in the speaker", reflects the age-old tendency to equate the meaning of a person's words with the momentary contents of his mind. If an image of red accompanies the word "red", that is its meaning. If no image typically accompanies the word "wrong", but a feeling of disapproval or horror does, then that is its meaning. Thesis and antithesis then form a dichotomy such as Wittgenstein alluded to in the *Investigations* (§317): "Misleading parallel: the expression of pain is a cry—the expression of thought, a proposition." For typical descriptivists, an ethical utterance is the latter sort of expression; it expresses a thought. For Ayer it is the former. Neither attends sufficiently to the background of the utterance, for instance to the reasons for calling something wrong, or includes such reasoning or the criteria followed within the meaning of the moral term. So Wittgenstein would say to both: "Take a *wider* look round."[4] "Only in the stream of thought and life do words have meaning."[5]

Indulgence in theories and counter-theories, theses and countertheses, generally stems from similar unreflectiveness, not about words' use in the language, but about one's own use of words in this language-game of theorizing. It would be wise to ask: How do accurate theories and theses, which are thought to be common, differ from accurate definitions, which are thought to be rare? The accuracy of a definition requires that expressions be found whose conceptual borders coincide, and that is seldom possible. The accuracy of a universal thesis or theory, on the other hand, requires that a given description be verified in all members of a class of things (e.g., all propositions, if the theory is about propositions, or all names, all religions, etc.). Yet the class of referents is specified by a general expression, simple or composite, so that the same problem recurs: the boundaries of the designating expression must coincide with those of the describing expression, and this can be achieved or at least approximated only in the exact sciences, by reason of the whole stream of life—measures, instruments, agreed procedures, collective observations, mathematical calculi, etc.— within which scientific expressions occur. Outside of the exact sciences, borders cannot generally be gotten to coincide with sufficient precision to justify a theory or thesis.

Thus Ayer's attempt, and not merely his result, seems mistaken. Moral discourse is far too varied to be captured in any one formula. Yet, like most antitheses, this one of Ayer's is worth reflecting on. Truth often appears nearer the surface in an antithesis than it does in the rejected thesis.

First let us attend more closely to the word "feeling", which recurs so frequently in Ayer's account. The way he uses the term suggests something momentary accompanying the speaker's words. Yet he also speaks of disapproval, and disapproval is no such "feeling", though there are feelings of disapproval, just as there are feelings of hope or despair. A word like "grief", "hope", or "approval", as Wittgenstein remarked, "describes a pattern which recurs, with different variations, in the weave of our life"[6]; and feelings are but one strand in that weave. To discover the full truth in an emotive theory of moral discourse, therefore, it is necessary to consider *emotions*, not just feelings.

Wittgenstein indicated one important variation in the weave when he observed: "Among emotions the directed might be distinguished from the undirected. Fear *at* something, joy *over* something."[7] But also vague, undefined fears. The cases form a continuum; for instance:

1. "As I awoke, I had the impression that something dreadful was going to happen. The fear stayed with me all day." (No target)

2. "It was my first flight, and I was frightened." (Not of anything very definite, but of what might happen. Of accidents.)

3. A child afraid of the dark. (Someone might say that the child is really afraid of what may be in the dark, much as the fearful passenger is nervous about what may happen to the plane. But would the child be equally afraid of a shiny cloud where visibility is equally low? The darkness itself is fearful.)

4. A large dog runs out, barking, showing its teeth. (In this case there is no doubt what is the target of the child's fear.)

"We should distinguish," Wittgenstein further observed, "between the object of fear and the cause of fear."[8] Miss Anscombe illustrates the distinction as follows: "A child saw a bit of red stuff on a turn in a stairway and asked what it was. He thought his nurse told him it was a bit of Satan and felt dreadful fear of it. (No doubt she said it was a bit of satin.) What he was frightened of was the bit of stuff; the cause of his fright was his nurse's remark. The object of fear may be the cause of fear, but as Wittgenstein remarks, is not *as such* the cause of fear. (A hideous face appearing at the window would of course be both cause and object, and hence the two are easily confused.)"[9]

These examples suggest another important distinction. We would hardly say that the face was a *reason* for fearing it, but we would say that the nurse's remark was a reason for the child's fear of the satin. Emotions are sometimes mere instinctive reactions; other times they are motivated, in a more or less conscious, rational manner. Here too there is a continuum of cases, for instance:

1. A childhood incident, long forgotten, makes a person fearful (he knows not why) of a present acquaintance, whose voice resembles that of a man who frightened him then.

2. An examiner inspires fear through his severe expression. The expression is not reflected on, but is at least observed, whereas the similarity of voices was not.

3. The person being examined not only notes the examiner's severe expression, but recalls his reputation for severity, so fears the more.

4. He has read the man's writings, disagrees with them, feels sure he will have to express his disagreement, so feels still more apprehensive. The issues in question may be as complex as you please. There is thus no limit to the amount of cognitive backing an emotion may have.

For these reasons Ayer's repeated use of the word "feeling" is misleading. It tends to obscure the objective dimensions of emotions—their targets and their reasons—and therefore the large element of truth in the view he opposed. Morality is objective in both these ways. People approve and disapprove of given actions; their attitudes have targets. And they approve and disapprove for reasons, often complex, highly cognitive ones. But in ethics, too, these factors vary. Though moral judgments characteristically have both targets and reasons, think for instance of the injunction "Good is to be done, evil avoided." As we speak of free-floating anxiety or fear, so we might speak of free-floating morality.

I can think of no more helpful single model, therefore, combining the truth in both objective and subjective views of ethics, than an emotion with a target and reasons. Yet the model is merely that—a helpful term of comparison, which throws light on the facts of moral discourse by way not only of similarities, but also of dissimilarities. It is time now to consider some of the latter.

First, one might say that moral discourse is grammatically as well as factually objective, whereas emotive expressions are not. As a first hint at the complex contrast I have in mind, here is a comparison: imagine a situation in which one person asks another "Do you feel too hot?" and, a bit later, "Is the room too hot?" The two questions may be pragmatically equivalent, and so may the answers, but the surface grammar[10] of the first puts the accent on the person, whereas the second puts it on the room. Passing to emotions, we might distinguish similarly between the child's fear and the fearful darkness, between "I am afraid of it" and "It's frightful." Finally, with regard to actions, we have "I approve of it" and "It's good," or "I disapprove of it" and "It's wrong." When we speak of moral discourse, we have the latter type of expression principally in mind, not the former, whereas discussion of emotions reverses the emphasis. Doubtless this fact of surface grammar, along with the elements of depth grammar already mentioned, accounts in large part for the traditional insistence on the objectivity of ethics. Constantly, invisibly, profoundly, the surface of language does affect our thinking in just such ways.

Note that I am not reducing the statement "It's wrong" to "I disapprove of it." That would be as foolish as reducing, "It's hot" to "I feel hot." The very comparison used precludes such a reduction. If anything, my remarks point in the other direction—to the fact that ethical discourse resembles "It's hot" more than it does "I feel hot." However, for the moment, here at the start of my list, I am concerned only with the surface dissimilarity between emotive and ethical expressions. I wish to point out only certain evident differences in surface grammar, for instance the fact that moral attributes, unlike emotions, are attributed to actions as well as to persons; and that even those applied to both are applied primarily to actions, secondarily to persons, a person being judged moral or immoral, just or unjust, and so on, insofar as his actions are moral or immoral, just or unjust, charitable, or uncharitable, etc., and not vice versa. A psychologist or sociologist asks typically, "Which actions do you approve, which disapprove?" A moralist asks typically, "What actions are right, which wrong?" At least the *surface* grammar of morals is more objective than that of emotions.

As for "depth grammar," it might seem that at the point now reached in our attempt to discover the synthetic truth in Ayer's antithesis, only the step from "It's frightful" to "It's hot" still separates us from the traditional thesis position. So let us examine that gap more closely. In what does the difference consist? Mere surface grammar tempts one to reply, "The heat is really in the hot room whereas the fear isn't in the dark room." However, in terms of immediate experience, the latter may be as thoroughly invested with our fear as the former is with heat. Phenomenologically, the union is complete. "*Things* are beautiful and ugly, lovely and hateful, dull and illuminated, attractive and repulsive. Stir and thrill in us is as much theirs as is length, breadth and thickness."[11] Only grammar and philosophy cut the two apart—the emotion and its object. And here, where our concern is meaning, not theory, we must for the moment ignore both sorts of cuts and examine instead the stream of life within which expressions such as "frightful" and "hot" are immersed.

Experientially speaking, it does not seem, however, that moral objects are invested with our approval and disapproval to quite the same degree. For they are typically actions, not dogs or dark rooms, and usually are actions contemplated in the future, not concrete particulars before our eyes. Of course we do fear the Ides of March or a raise in the rent; fear, too, can point ahead, and can take events for its target, as well as objects. And moral judgments, for their part, can relate to concrete actions of the past or present. But they never have mere objects—spiders or bolts of lightning—as their targets, whereas emotions often do. And moral judgments point toward the abstract future still more frequently than emotions do. Thus, moral targets being less paradigmatically objective, moral qualifications such as right and wrong dwell in them with less phenomenological immediacy than fearfulness does in a hideous face, or loveliness in a loved person, or heat in a hot room.

However, to a considerable extent this contrast is an illusion generated by surface grammar, as appears if we turn to the second aspect of objectivity, that is, to the reasons rather than the targets. The first thing to notice is that lessened objectivity in the target brings a cognitive increase. One may start back in terror from a rattlesnake, without giving it a thought, but a future action must be conceived. And the more complex the object, the more reflection generally goes into its evaluation. We simply "like" the shape of someone's nose, but "approve" of birth control or capital punishment. For the latter we have reasons, the same that underlie our declarations that birth control or capital punishment is right or wrong.

Second, the arguments adduced for or against a contemplated action usually lead at last to aspects or effects which we simply recognize or regard as good or bad without further reason: food, clothing, pleasure, friendship, health, worship, recreation, beauty. Or, more concretely (to make the connection with previous examples unmistakable): light in the dark room, a chain for the barking dog, removal of the hideous face from the window, a different examiner, etc. In final analysis, such is the stuff of which most moral judgments are made. So, one way or the other, the immediate objectivity which frequently characterizes emotions characterizes morality too. If the values or disvalues are mere effects of a contemplated action, the morality of the action seems less intrinsic to it, less localized in the act itself; if they are aspects of the action, the moral target resembles more closely the frightful bulldog, terrible accident, adorable child. It is because the wounds, the screams, the destruction were so horrible (so horrifying) that the Vietnam War, for instance, was judged by many to be immoral. But these *were* the war; they were among its ingredients. Thus the war itself was horrible, and calling it wrong was hardly distinguishable from calling it horrible, when, as was often the case, no more complex reasons were considered.

To sum up now: (1) emotions generally have a target, and so do moral judgments; (2) an emotion often seems to be as much in the object as in the subject, and the same is true at least of the motives for moral judgments and often of their targets as well; (3) both the targets and the causes (reasons) of moral judgments tend to be still more cognitive than those of emotions, though both fluctuate widely; (4) talk of emotions is subject-centered in its surface grammar, whereas moral discourse is target-centered. All these are reasons for calling the latter objective, and cognitive.

Note the special prominence this analysis gives to the reasons for moral judgments. The particular facts and things cited for or against an action contribute objectivity to a judgment of its morality as the individual bits of colored stone give color to a mosaic; the evil or good is there, alive, in the concrete determinations and ramifications of the act. And it is the piecing together of all these aspects which calls reason into play, more than in the genesis of emotive utterances. *Reasons* are the chief source of both objectivity and cognitivity in ethical statements, setting them off from mere exclamations. Hence, when I come in later chapters to examine specific moral teachings, I shall attend to the reasoning employed or implied, as a chief indication of the statement's meaning or lack of meaning.

"But," someone may well object, "do the reasons belong to

the *meaning* of a statement? When I state a conclusion, do I state the reasons too? As invalid arguments often lead to true conclusions, may not incoherent reasoning lead to quite meaningful conclusions?"

This objection shows the need of Wittgenstein's distinction[12] between criteria, which belong to the very meaning of an expression, and symptoms, which do not. The former form the basis of agreed rules which permit communication; the latter are open to dispute by those playing the game. If, for instance, one person hears thunder and says it is raining nearby, another person may question his conclusion. Thunder is a mere symptom of rain, a clue, a helpful bit of evidence that might conceivably be wrong. But if one person sees drops coming down from clouds and another person accepts these facts but questions whether it is raining, he is no longer speaking the English language. This is simply what people call rain, and there's an end to it. It is what thunder is evidence for.

A similar distinction appears in moral reasoning. If you want to find what a moralist means by his terms, see where his arguments not only tend, but end. If, for instance, he refuses to go beyond the will of God, he is a voluntarist; for him the terms "right" and "wrong" simply *mean* what God commands, permits, or forbids. That's rock-bottom in his language-game with these terms. If another moralist cites basic principles in favor of a permission or prohibition, then supports the principles through reference to values, the principles are mere symptoms, the values are the ultimate criteria, and so on.

For various reasons, such an analysis may seem to exaggerate the diversity of moral meanings. I shall return to this misgiving later, in Chapter Five, so will only mention here that pragmatic and psychological aspects, rather than cognitive, account in large part for the impression that moral expressions have fairly constant meanings. Whatever his motives, the person who says of an action "It's wrong" does not like it. And whatever the grounds for the utterance or the information it conveys, it has the further force of "Don't do it!" But were

"It's wrong" simply equivalent to "I don't like it" or "Don't do it" or both together, morality might be matter for Church legislation, but not for Church teaching. It is the factual components of their sense which make moral statements something more than mere commands or expressions of approval and disapproval; and the factual components—the arguments and the evidence—vary considerably.

Still, concerning moral ultimates there is more agreement than is generally supposed. Argumentation typically leads back to basics such as I mentioned earlier: pleasure and pain, health and sickness, companionship and isolation, knowledge and ignorance, sight and blindness, power and weakness, life and death, and so on. Frequently it stops at evident symptoms; if, for instance, someone cites the danger of war as a reason against some line of action, he need hardly mention that were war to result someone might get killed; or if someone argues against the SST on the grounds of sonic boom, he need hardly mention that the discomfort of excessively loud noise and fatigue from shortened sleep are evils to be avoided. On such things everyone agrees. Those who disagree, who for instance consider pain a desirable thing, are confined in the same institutions with those who believe they are Geronimo or that the Japanese beetles are after them.

Disagreement on moral matters derives principally, therefore, from factors such as the following (together with their repercussions in tradition, upbringing, and so on, which may accentuate diversity still further): (1) different weighting given to factors accepted by all as values, or accepted by all as disvalues; (2) failure to note all the values or disvalues involved, some noting some, some others; (3) disagreement concerning the extent to which the values or disvalues noted would be realized by the contemplated action; (4) in addition to widely divergent views of God, man, and the universe, general ignorance, even on the part of the best-educated, of the enormous body of concrete fact, and of the various sociological, psychological, economic, biological, physical and other laws required for an accurate estimate of what values are involved to what extent in any line of action, even the most specific; (5) general unawareness of the logic of this language-game, as of all others, together with the special complexity of this one, so that even if they possessed all the requisite information people would still handle it with quite varying degrees of success (their moral reasoning and conclusions would vary still more widely than their bridge games).

There is a further, important sense, therefore, in which we might say that moral discourse is objective. Objectivity, in one main sense of the term, is gauged by common agreement: the event which only one person reports is a dream, a mirage, an illusion, delirium tremens, a lie, a hallucination, or what have you, but not objective fact, not if no one else around had any sight or sound of it. The thing we agree to is an object, a fact. Similarly, I have argued, there is a great deal of grass-roots agreement in ethics, at the level of meaning, despite the far wider and more thorough disagreement on all higher levels. The difference between the common base and the debated superstructure resembles that between, say, assertions about the color of visible objects, on the one hand, and scientific hypotheses, on the other, which, if they turn out to be false, are replaced by others, with little or no shift in the concepts.[13]

Whatever truth this assessment contains can hardly fail to have important consequences for the analysis of moral meaning. If the reasons for moral pronouncements are the aspect deserving most attention, and if ultimate reasons deserve most attention of all, then a foundation common to most of mankind is of utmost importance. And such are the items I have cited. As *common* values and disvalues, they are likely to affect many moral judgments. As common *values* and *disvalues*, that is, things considered good or bad in themselves, they are likely to serve as ultimate, decisive reasons. It can hardly be said that a solid bedrock of agreement underlies our ethical judgments,[14] but at least there is an undulating *terra firma* on which most of us, ethical aviators and frogmen apart, tend to walk most of the time.

In further illustration and support of this suggestion, whose significance is now clear, consider some simple examples of disagreement cited by Stevenson. Since his purpose was different from mine, my use of his list may allay suspicions of biased selection: "Mrs. A has social aspirations, and wants to move with the elite. Mr. A is easy-going, and loyal to his old friends. They accordingly disagree about what guests they will invite to their party. The curator of the museum wants to buy pictures by contemporary artists; some of his advisers prefer the purchase of old masters. They disagree. John's mother is concerned about the dangers of playing football, and doesn't want him to play. John, even though he agrees (in belief) about the dangers, wants to play anyhow. Again, they disagree. These examples, like the previous one, involve an opposition of attitudes, and differ only in that the attitudes in question are a little stronger, and are likely to be defended more seriously."[15]

It seems likely that in each of these cases the weighting would differ, not the values or disvalues. A boy, for instance, does not secretly desire bruises, sprains, and broken bones whereas his mother dreads them. Nor does she see no value at all in football. It is just that she sees less value in it than he does. Hence the disagreement about whether he should play. It seems equally probable that the curator of the museum would see *some* value in old masters, and his advisers see *some* value in contemporary works, and that Mrs. A is not completely insensitive to the value of old friends nor Mr. A to the amenities of society. The coefficient varies, not the sign. It is this situation I had in mind when I spoke of an undulating *terra firma*.

As for my earlier remarks about differences in argument which reveal differences in meaning, it should be clear by now that the differences I had in mind were generic, between diverse, perhaps incompatible approaches, and not differences of detail within a single perspective. It is one thing to agree that a, b, c, and d are values and e, f, g, and h disvalues, and quite another thing to base one's moral judgments in general, or some judgment in particular, on reference to such values and disvalues and their conjunction. People sometimes adopt other frameworks, and the meanings of their terms are then affected, as well as their verdicts. But insofar as ultimate reference is regularly made to a fairly consistent set of values and disvalues, moral meanings remain relatively stable. They may be little affected by the fact that one person cites values which another overlooks; or paints a different picture of the facts; or stresses man's natural end whereas another speaks of authenticity; etc. For meaning, the decisive criteria are the ultimate ones.

If there is all this agreement at the level of meaning, despite confusion and disagreement on the level of reasoning and moral hypothesis, it might seem that moral judgments are relatively safe from any charge of meaninglessness. But that would be true, at most, of the mass of mankind left to their instincts. For the extensive parallel between physical and moral judgments holds in this respect, too, that among the minority of mankind given to speculation, especially philosophers and theologians, much less harmony prevails concerning foundations. "The philosopher," wrote Wittgenstein, "is not a citizen of any community of ideas. That is what makes him into a philosopher."[16] Thus some have claimed that the red we see is really a part of our brains; or an idea put there by God; or the product of an unknowable X which alone is really red, if anything is; or the isomorphic correlate of an extramental cause; and so on. The familiar table of common sense becomes an idea we share with the divine mind, a geometrical skeleton fleshed of its secondary qualities, a set of sensations we might have if we had some head-moving sensations in the right direction, and so on. And if it is thus in the green wood, what in the dry? Tables and colors are child's-play compared with morals.

Looking forward, therefore, to the applications which lie ahead, we can conclude that: (1) there is a serious possibility of ultimate incoherence in moral discourse; (2) moral reasoning is the chief indication of moral meaning (at least where explicit, truly clarifying definitions are lacking, as is usually the case); (3) most important of all are ultimate reasons, whose acceptance as reasons (in that particular author or language-game) neither receives nor requires further justification. Looking backward from the same points to the initial alternative, between the blanket acceptance of moral statements as informative and their rejection as emotive, we can now see why the appropriate answer is not a compromise admission that some are informative and some aren't and we just need to sort them out. Even the child who declares "That's naughty!" will reply, when asked for a reason, "Mommy said so." And on the level of magisterial pronouncements, there are invariably reasons, generally complex ones, on the authors' part, and corresponding effects on the recipients' part, at least among readers belonging to the same community of thought as those who penned the statements. Given sufficient conceptual affinity between reader and writer, hearer and speaker, any formula which results naturally from a given set of beliefs and considerations will beget kindred beliefs and considerations in those who read or hear it. That is why till now I have said so little about information and so much about reasons.

In this I have followed the example of Ayer himself, who paid relatively little attention to the information actually conveyed by statements and much more to their verification, that is, to the reasons for or against them. If a person looks out the window, sees a drizzle coming down, and later says, "It rained this morning," his hearer will not go through the same process nor visualize the exact amount of rain, nor necessarily imagine anything at all; but there will be considerable correspondence between his resulting belief and what the speaker saw. He will not know just when the rain fell, nor how abundantly and extensively, but he will know that some water came down some time that morning somewhere in the vicinity. And so it is with moral statements. If one utilitarian tells another utilitarian that euthanasia is all right, the other has a rough idea what configuration of fact and value is indicated. If the hearer's ethical concepts differ considerably from the speaker's, the message will be correspondingly dim. And if all the hearer shares with the speaker is a set of ultimate values such as those referred to above, there may be no communication at all. They no longer speak the same language. The borderline thus crossed is not that between informative and emotive, but between meaningful and meaningless.

For like-minded hearers, however, the same utterance may be perfectly meaningful.[17] So it is with magisterial statements. Non-Christians or even non-Catholics may not readily understand them, but for those within the fold their meaning may be clear enough. And yet it may not be. The reasoning behind the statements and implied or expressed in their presentation may be more or less incoherent. And even within the same community of thought, wide variations may exist, rendering not only agreement but understanding difficult. Such differences have become more pronounced within the contemporary Church, but they are not new.

As an illuminating paradigm of intra-community diversity, consider this exchange in a synagogue of Galilee: "A man with a withered hand was there. And they were watching him, whether he cured on the Sabbath, that they might accuse him. And he said to the man with the withered hand, 'Stand forth in the midst.' And he said to them, 'Is it lawful on the Sabbath to do good, or to do evil? to save a life, or to destroy it?' But they kept silence. And looking round upon them with anger, and being grieved at the blindness of their hearts, he said to the man, 'Stretch forth thy hand.' And he stretched it forth, and his hand was restored. But the Pharisees went out and immediately took counsel with the Herodians against him, how they might do away with him" (Mk. 3, 1-6).

The contrast is familiar: man for the Sabbath versus the Sabbath for man, or, more generally: law versus values—an absolute formula, valid in all cases, versus absolute values and disvalues, to be considered whenever they arise. Since the same contrast has continued through the centuries and dominated Christian ethics, it deserves closer examination in this paradigm confrontation.

Jesus's attitude, which should be ours, is summed up in the words: "I have come that they may have life and may have it more abundantly." His account of the Last Judgment, in Matthew 25, and his living of the lesson, as reported by the gospels, indicate the broad sense we should give the word "life": life of the body, life of the mind, the heart, the emotions, the whole man. For the blind saw, the lame walked, the lepers were cleansed, the deaf heard, the dead rose, and the poor had the gospel preached to them. And when he came on this cripple in the synagogue, no mere precept stood in his way: "Stretch forth thy hand!" Let him have life. The corporal and spiritual works of mercy have perpetuated his mission, and have refracted as in a spectrum the simple injunction of St. Paul: "The whole Law is fulfilled in one word: Thou shalt love thy neighbor as thyself" (Gal. 5, 14). Towards ourselves our attitude is: "May I have life and have it more abundantly." Christian moral teaching directs us to wish the same for all. May they too have life, here and hereafter, in all its fullness.

Yet there is another trend, the one exemplified by Christ's adversaries in the synagogue. They held doggedly to the precept at all costs because, they said, it was a divine command, so not to be contravened. Were they voluntarists, then? And was the God of Israel, for them at least, a mere lawgiver and not shepherd of his flock? Was the Sabbath precept an arbitrary fiat, without rhyme or reason? No, but the explanation was of an entirely different genre. As the alliance which the Sabbath had come to represent was a historical reality, so the Sabbath itself had a story: in the sacred books and therefore in the minds of devout Jews, it was connected with Israel's deliverance from Egypt (Deut. 5, 15) and with the story of creation: "Remember to keep the Sabbath holy . . . for in six days the Lord made the heavens, the earth, and the sea, together with all that is in them, but rested on the seventh day; that is how the Lord came to bless the seventh day and to hallow it" (Ex. 20, 8-11). These connections, too, would tend to make the precept absolute, inviolable. If Jahweh himself did no work on the Sabbath, who is mere man to do differently?

The incompatibility between this viewpoint and Christ's took dramatic, visible form in that tense moment when he asked, "Is it lawful to do good on the Sabbath?", and they remained silent but raged inwardly. Their motives were complex, it is true, and their reasoning was not always consistent; but the contrast holds: he on the one hand and they on the other represented two distinct systems of moral reasoning within which the very meaning of the terms differed.[18] So long as the division is as clear-cut on each side as there in the synagogue, communication may be difficult from side to side, but at least on each side there is enough consistency so that Pharisees can talk with Pharisees and Christians with Christians. But suppose now, to take a realistic last look at our paradigm, that the followers of Christ are former Pharisees or disciples of Pharisees, trying to cross over from one side to the other. Their confusion may be considerable. Or suppose that they are Greeks or disciples of Greeks, addicted to definitions and eternal truths, or Romans and disciples of Romans, habituated to codes of law, or scientists and admirers of science, wedded to scientific formulae. Or suppose that they are unreflective people still more prone to simplification and confusion than a Socrates, when he went in pursuit of essences. As the tributaries flow in, and the currents and cross-currents grow strong and treacherous, and the problems get more and more complex, it may become exceedingly difficult to keep the original dichotomy clearly in focus: man for precepts versus precepts for man; absolute formulae versus absolute values and disvalues. The possibility of ultimate incoherence becomes all too real.

I shall return to this theme in the final chapter, when concrete case studies have cast sharper light on the issues.

CHAPTER FOUR

Muddle or Mystery

T his chapter will be a stepping stone: adding philosophical and theological examples to the simpler, everyday ones in Chapters Two and Three, and focussing more sharply on the problematic area where meaningful and meaningless converge, it will thereby provide proximate preparation for the treatment of magisterial statements in Chapter Five. Suspect samples will be cleared and unsuspected ones incriminated, in ways which can guide and clarify discussion there, when the question is finally faced: What of Church teaching?

1. But on his journey, as he was approaching Damascus, a sudden light flashed around him from heaven, and he fell to the ground. Then he heard a voice saying to him, "Saul! Saul! Why do you persecute me?" "Who are you, sir?" he asked. "I am Jesus whom you are persecuting." (Acts 9, 3-5)

The gospels provide numerous leads to the meaning of these concluding words, "whom you are persecuting." From their pages there emerges the picture of one who achieved the ideal he preached and in literal truth loved his every neighbor as a man loves himself, feeling each one's joys and sorrows, therefore, as though they were his own. "Insofar as you did it to one of the humblest of these brothers of mine," he could therefore tell Paul too, "you did it to me" (Mt. 25, 40). Would the words have been just as true, though, would they have had an identical meaning, had non-Christians been the ones suffering at Paul's hands? It was not to just anyone that Jesus said, "He who hears you hears me." He did not say indiscriminately to the whole human race, "Wherever two or more of you are gathered together, there am I in your midst." Not everyone is a member of the mystical body described by Paul.

So we are back in the situation of the diviner.[1] If a water diviner said, "I feel water twenty feet down," we might surmise that he felt a tickle in the soles of his feet which he had found was associated with water at just that depth. And we have felt tickles. But we would probably suspect that his sensation differed somewhat from any we had experienced. We might even wonder, in the Wittgensteinian manner, whether he was referring to a feeling at all. So too in the present case we might imagine that the words of Christ indicate that degree and universality of charity to which all are called and which most have experienced to some degree. But we are inclined to suspect a fuller, more mysterious explanation: not just the superhuman humanity of the Son of Man, but the whole wide mystery of his relation to the nascent Church. The cognitive pattern, once again, is an indefinite conjunction, from which the intended referent may be wholly or partially missing.

Let us move on now to a case which is more clearly transcendent, yet where human reason can still suggest considerable articulation of the sense. Paradoxically, it will appear that the very transcendence of the statement not only explains its interest but guarantees its sense.

2.   But if one of you asks his father for a
            loaf, will he hand him a stone? or for a
            fish, will he for a fish hand him a ser-
            pent? Or if he asks for an egg, will he
            hand him a scorpion? Therefore, if you,
            evil as you are, know how to give good
            gifts to your children, how much more
            will your heavenly Father give the
            Good Spirit to those who ask him! (Lk.
            11, 11-13)

But what if, being in dire need, we ask our heavenly Father
for aid and receive none? Doesn't the inference implicit in
Christ's words then work in reverse? Mustn't we conclude that
God does not love us, that he is not a loving father? And if we
refuse to draw that conclusion, what meaning is then left to the
statement? Hasn't it died the death of a thousand qualifications? Such is the reasoning of Antony Flew, in a well-known
and much-discussed article:

Now it often seems to people who are not religious as if
there was no conceivable event or series of events the occurrence of which would be admitted by sophisticated religious people to be a sufficient reason for conceding
"There wasn't a God after all" or "God does not really
love us then." Someone tells us that God loves us as a father loves his children. We are reassured. But then we see
a child dying of inoperable cancer of the throat. His earth-
ly father is driven frantic in his efforts to help, but his
Heavenly Father reveals no obvious sign of concern. Some
qualification is made—God's love is "not a merely human
love" or it is "an inscrutable love," perhaps—and we realize that such sufferings are quite compatible with the truth
of the assertion that "God loves us as a father (but, of
course, . . .)." We are reassured again. But then perhaps
we ask: What is this assurance of God's (appropriately

qualified) love worth, what is this apparent guarantee really a guarantee against? Just what would have to happen not merely (morally and wrongly) to tempt but also (logically and rightly) to entitle us to say, "God does not love us" or even "God does not exist"?[2]

Flew's argument is not just a piece of polemics. It articulates the problem of evil as people experience it in their lives; it gives logical expression to doubts many believers have felt. Therein lies much of its significance. A problem cannot be dealt with until it is brought into the light and clearly stated; and the problem Flew has clearly stated badly needs to be dealt with. How badly appears from the answers to his challenge, which were on the whole remarkably unsuccessful, though their authors were trained philosophers and theologians. If they experienced such difficulties, what success is an ordinary Christian likely to have?

In one crucial respect, the believer's problem tends to differ from that raised by Flew: the believer is tempted to doubt that God is a loving Father, whereas Flew wondered whether the belief is even meaningful. "He was suggesting that the believer's earlier statement had been so eroded by qualification that it was no longer an assertion at all."[3] Thus:

The challenge . . . ran like this. Some theological utterances seem to, and are intended to, provide explanations or express assertions. Now an assertion, to be an assertion at all, must claim that things stand thus and thus; *and not otherwise*. Similarly an explanation, to be an explanation at all, must explain why this particular thing occurs; *and not something else*. Those last clauses are crucial. And yet sophisticated religious people—or so it seemed to me—are apt to overlook this, and tend to refuse to allow, not merely that anything actually does occur, but that anything conceivably could occur, which would count against their theological assertions and explanations. But in so far as they do this their supposed explanations are actually bogus, and their seeming assertions are really vacuous.[4]

I find it surprising that the basic ambiguity of Flew's formulation has escaped so many people's notice. "Just what would have to happen," he demands, "to entitle us to say 'God does not love us'?" But how is this question to be taken? Does it ask for some single event or isolated series of events, or rather for a detailed, comprehensive account of the entire universe and its course, with all causal connections laid bare? Flew clearly envisages the former, yet only the latter is relevant. For the assertion of God's love is not a statement about isolated facts but about his providence for the world as a whole; it means that any evil we may choose to consider is permitted by reason of its place within the universal scheme of things. This is not only the view expressed by reference to God as a loving father, but the one required to connect such expressions with their ordinary use when, for instance, we say that a human father loves his child. For a loving father is not one who never refuses what his child wants and perhaps clamors for, nor one who never causes the child to suffer, but one who looks to his overall good, along with that of others—wife, children, neighbors, and friends.

A young child, let us suppose, becomes excited as guests start to arrive and asks to stay up for the party. "Just this once," he pleads. But his father insists on his going to bed. Why? Because the boy needs his sleep. Because his presence would displease one of the guests or put a damper on the party. For the sake of regularity in the child's life, and so as not to favor his every whim, with the results that would have in the long-run on the development of his character. And so on. That is, the father bases his decision on facts, values, and causal connections of which he is aware but which lie outside the small child's ken. The youngster does not know the guests or what they plan to do or how his presence would affect their evening. He has probably forgotten the effect on his disposition and behavior the last time he stayed up late, and perhaps never connected the way he felt the day after with his lack of sleep the night before. And of course he knows nothing about child psychology, or the connection between early training and adult personality. The very word "personality" means practically nothing to him, that level of values, so decisive in his father's considerations, having barely appeared on his horizon. So the child is in no position to judge his father's love on the basis of this one decision or of any combination. A smile, a kiss, a tone of voice—such are the bases of his trust, not complicated calculations of his father's motivation and strategy.

So it is with Christians. They have not deciphered the workings of the universe, but they have seen God's love in the person of Christ. And their resulting belief in God's love is like that of the child. They trust that he, in his wisdom, knows what is best for us and in his power does what depends on him to bring it about. As in the case of a truly discerning father, this may mean letting us lead our own lives, make our own mistakes, and suffer the consequences. But it also means helping us in all ways he knows to be consistent with our genuine growth and happiness. He allows the prodigal to depart but welcomes him back with open arms. The prodigal, clearly, does not possess his father's wisdom. He is blind not only to connections, but even to many values. That is why he is in no position to deny his father's love on the strength of any one event. He cannot say, for instance: "My father saw where I was headed, but he did not stop me. How then can he love me?" He can only say, "I wonder why he let me go." We are in a similar position when we ask, "Why does God allow this child with cancer to suffer?" We don't know, but our not knowing does not disprove God's love, any more than our failure to find his method disproves the statement of Professor M, in Chapter Two (#8). Or rather, should we not recognize our limitations far more readily when comparing ourselves with God than when comparing ourselves with a scientist, however brilliant, and when envisaging a plan for the universe and not merely a technique for controlling nuclear fusion?

This is not just the answer of common sense, based on the

everyday use of terms like "love" and "good." It is the traditional approach to the problem. So one wonders why it was so consistently ignored in the answers to Flew, or by Flew himself. One explanation, no doubt, is that analytic philosophy has tended to make sense dependent on the possibility of verification or falsification. Most philosophers have abandoned the attempt to formulate an acceptable version of the verification principle, tying sense to the possibility of empirical confirmation. And Popper's falsification principle has not generally been converted into a criterion of meaning; a statement which cannot be empirically falsified simply does not count as a scientific one. But what is shunned in theory may be favored in practice; a principle which is seen to be unacceptable when explicitly formulated may nevertheless remain operative in individual cases. When the principle goes underground in this way it cannot be refuted, but the same counter-examples may be cited which would invalidate it if stated. The case of Professor M is such a counter-example. So let us consider it again, this time in terms of verification and falsification.

Concerning the professor's statement, three things should be observed: (1) No event would falsify it. More specifically, no failure of a proposed procedure would falsify it. If some researcher thought he had discovered the secret of controlling nuclear fusion, then found the method did not work, this result would leave the truth and meaningfulness of the professor's claim untouched. He did not say fusion could be controlled in *that* way. (2) There is no known procedure for working out the answer or testing his statement. Thus the example differs basically from those that were frequently cited against the verification principle. It was suggested, for instance, that we lack the means to check on the statement, "There is life on at least one other planet in the universe," but that the statement is meaningful, nonetheless. In answer, defenders of the verification principle readily modified it to read: "A statement is meaningful only if there is some *conceivable* way of verifying it empirically." Spaceships may not yet be available which could take us on a tour of the universe, but we know what we would have to do to verify the statement about life on the other planets. In fact we are already in the process of checking the nearest planets. There is, however, no comparable procedure for verifying the professor's statement. Hit-and-miss is not a method. (3) It is conceivable that further investigation would reveal the impossibility of controlling fusion; it might be seen to involve two things which are incompatible.[5] With respect to divine providence, on the contrary, it seems evident that there can be no incompatibility, any more than in the case of a father's care for his children. The only situation which would preclude choice of the better for a family or for a universe would be one in which all possible combinations of events would turn out to be equally good or equally bad; and that is clearly not the case. For "good" and "bad" point to values and disvalues which clearly could be proportionately increased or decreased. Were it not so, all moral deliberation would be a waste of time; a basic error would underly all attempts to better the world in any respect. Thus, if anything, Christian belief in divine providence stands in a more favorable position with respect to verification than does the professor's statement, and I doubt that Flew would call that vacuous. If he did, one might legitimately suspect that the vacuity lay elsewhere.

In his biography of Wittgenstein, Norman Malcolm recounts a story which clarifies the point at which we have arrived: "The philosopher and psychologist, G. F. Stout, came to Cambridge for a brief visit and Wittgenstein invited him to tea. . . . Stout said to Wittgenstein that he had heard that Wittgenstein had something interesting and important to say about *verification*, and that he would like very much to know about it. Both of them knew that Stout had to leave very shortly to catch a train and Wittgenstein would not ordinarily, as he told me, have tried to make any kind of philosophical remark in such circumstances. But Stout's seriousness and genuine desire to understand Wittgenstein's teaching on this point so impressed him that he related to Stout the following parable: Imagine that there is a town in which the policemen are required to obtain information from each inhabitant, e.g., his age, where he came from, and what work he does. A record is kept of this information and some use is made of it. Occasionally when a policeman questions an inhabitant he discovers that the latter does not do *any* work. [He is, for instance, a contemplative.] The policeman enters this fact on the record, because *this too* is a useful piece of information about the man!"[6]

Similarly, it is highly significant and instructive that belief in God's love, unlike belief in a scientific theory or a newspaper report, is neither verified nor falsified by any event or series of events. Were it otherwise, the belief would lose its interest. For a providence which was humanly testable and predictable would resemble the kind of exceptionless moral precepts which have come in for so much criticism of late. It would not adapt itself to the endlessly varied contexts and consequences, known to God alone, of actions and events, but would follow instead some fixed law, a law so simple (despite its covering *all* events!) that we could understand it, and so rigid that we would never need to envisage the possibility of an exception. For the moment an exception was admissible, for unknown reasons which lay outside the law, we would never know concerning any individual case whether it might not be an exception. That is, we would be back in the situation Flew indicates, unable to determine God's love from any single event. The absurdity of the alternative providence which I have just described shows plainly why we cannot empirically verify God's love in the way Flew requests, and why we should not want to be able to. It also reveals, indirectly, that belief in divine goodness makes excellent sense.

However, this question is, after all, one that even natural theologians have felt competent to discuss. What happens when we move to those truths which theologians have considered completely beyond human comprehension, the *"mysteria stricte dicta"* of traditional theology?

3. The following passage belongs to a text which was prepared

for discussion by the First Vatican Council but was never presented:

> Of all the mysteries that we profess in
> the light of faith, the supreme mystery
> is God himself, who is one in essence,
> three in persons, Father, Son, and Holy
> Spirit. According to the truth of the
> Catholic faith, the blessed Trinity is
> one God, because the essence or sub-
> stance common to the three persons is
> really and numerically one.[7]

The doctrine of the Trinity has been considered a "supreme mystery" in another sense too: it has been regarded as supremely mysterious. And so it is; but not for logical reasons. Not because it is a conceptual puzzle, but because it is a transcendent revelation. The doctrine is especially mysterious, it is often supposed, because of the apparent or near contradiction in speaking of only one nature but three persons. Non-believing philosophers surmise, perhaps, that here if anywhere is an example of theological nonsense. Believing Christians, on the other hand, sometimes imagine that the contradiction is patent but that they are called on, God helping, to believe contradictions too.

Whence this impression of contradiction, seeing that even the surface appearance of contradiction is lacking? It is understandable that some philosophers, forgetting about circles of circles, series of series, collections of collections, classes of classes, and so on, should suppose there is a patent contradiction in suggesting that one substance might consist of many substances. But in the present instance there is one *essence*, three *persons*. The words are not the same. So the explanation must be sought in depth grammar. People are familiar with a certain use of these terms and tend to model the new use on that. Where there are three human persons there are three individual essences. If the same connection held—if the terms had the same logic—in statements about the Trinity, a contradiction would indeed lurk beneath the surface. But of course the same logic does not hold and the words are not used in the same way. A formula like the one I quoted at the start must be traced back and interpreted by means of scriptural sayings concerning Father, Son, or Holy Spirit (immediately derived from the teaching of Christ, we may reasonably suppose, when not verbally identical with it); and these are to be compared with a statement such as that in Chapter Two, #7, describing colors to the congenitally blind. Taken strictly, that statement too ("Scarlet is like a trumpet note") would seem incoherent or implicitly contradictory. But of course the terms need not and should not be taken strictly. Scarlet is not like a trumpet note the way a bugle note or other *sound* is.

The similarities between a simple model like this color description on the one hand and a transcendent revelation on the other help to clarify the possibility of such revelation. But the dissimilarities, too, are instructive. Most immediately and evidently relevant to our present problem is the fact that when we describe colors to a blind person through comparisons with sounds, no misgivings arise about the meaningfulness of the descriptions, whereas such doubts do arise concerning the propositions in which we state revealed mysteries, for instance that of the Trinity of divine persons. This difference is connected with the fact that the numerical ratio is here reversed: instead of one blind and many sighted, there is now just one who sees and many who do not. So the one who sees uses their words, not his. Whereas the color term in "Scarlet is like a trumpet note" belongs to an area of language with which the blind man is only partially familiar, all the words of revelation are those of the blind; that is, they are terms with whose ordinary use the recipients are fully acquainted. So to achieve a clearer insight into the situation than the model in #7 permits, let us alter it appropriately and see what a description might look like which sought to convey some notion of colors to a blind person without using any color expressions.

We might start with the statement that in addition to sounds and tastes and smells there exist other properties which lie beyond the ken of our blind hearer. Like sounds, we add, they may be arranged in a continuum. But unlike sounds, the whole continuum may be simultaneously present to the observer. In fact a sighted person may simultaneously perceive several such continua (for instance several rainbows). This is likely to confuse the blind man, for none of his senses help him to conceive even one such continuum, much less several simultaneously perceived. A continuum of notes from the top of the scale to the bottom, played simultaneously, would yield just an indiscriminate blast of sound. To form a perceptible continuum, the notes would have to be played successively. Tastes, likewise, might conceivably pass without perceptible break from strawberry to cherry to rhubarb and so on; but that sequence, like the flow of violin notes or a series of smells, would be a temporal continuum, not a momentary datum. As for feelings of pain, heat, cold, hardness, and the like, we may, for instance, feel cold in the feet and hot in the face at the same time; but we have not gone through the experiment of carefully gradating the heat applied to our skin, from the top of our head to the tip of our toes. And even if we did attempt the experiment, it is doubtful whether the result would be a perceived continuum of degrees, ranging from hot to cold. Such assertions, therefore, about mysterious, transcendent properties arranged in multiple, simultaneous continua would naturally strike the blind man as a tissue of contradictions and it would take the full weight of the sighted majority to make him accept them as meaningful. The question is whether the word of a single witness will carry equal weight when he reveals still more transcendent mysteries.

4. If a scientist said, "I have found a way to control nuclear fusion," we would request an explanation. If our next-door neighbor declared, "I and the Father are one," we would be rather more insistent. Without further elucidation we would question not only the truth of his statement but also its mean-

ingfulness. When (and if) it is Christ, though, who speaks these same words, our attitude is different, especially if we accept in similarly traditional fashion the fact and sense of his claim to have seen the Father. We then class his statements with descriptions of colors for the blind. It is somewhat as though we were out rowing with a friend and he suddenly put aside his oars and gazed at his wrist. "What are you doing?" we ask. "Watching the astronauts on the moon," he replies. It would make a difference to the meaningfulness of his statement if he wore a TV set on his wrist.

Thus there is a basic difference between a revelation and a theory, between the statement of someone whose experience and knowledge transcend our own and an equally mystifying utterance of someone basically similar to ourselves. In the first case we trust not only the truth of what is said, but its meaningfulness, for basically similar reasons. The one who tells us of transcendent reality will, we feel sure, neither deceive us nor talk nonsense. In terms of the previous parallel, he will neither inaccurately describe scarlet as similar to the sound of wind in the pines nor nonsensically compare it to an isosceles triangle. But when an ordinary person utters the same words, we have no assurance on either score. That is why without further clarification, we can dismiss his utterance as vacuous. He owes us an explanation.

In subsequent samples, such will be my attitude. After three examples from revelation, illustrating the semantic and epistemological diversity in doctrines of faith, I pass now to three purely human doctrines, so become more exigent. None passes muster, yet each fails in its own interesting, typical way. Nonsense, too, comes in many forms. And some of its guises veil the underlying lack so cunningly that we hesitate to speak of nonsense. Intelligent people have made such statements.

Let us start with Arthur Vermeersch, S.J., who played a leading role in the preparation of *Casti Connubii*. A few years prior to that encyclical's condemnation of artificial contraception, which we shall examine anon, Vermeersch proposed the following formulation:

> Thesis VI: The onanistic use of mar-
> riage is intrinsically and gravely evil.[8]

Without attending to other problems, let us focus on the word "evil". As Chapter Three suggests and Vermeersch's argumentation makes clear,[9] we cannot presuppose that this term has a single common meaning and that it has the same sense here. But Vermeersch provides no explicit account of the meaning he intends. So we shall have to examine his reasons and see what sense they suggest. First he appeals to Scripture and the Fathers, but too briefly to be of any help. His argument from reason is fuller. "In the onanistic use of marriage," he writes, "one or both of the spouses . . . have intercourse in a way which deprives the act of its relation to the species and which refers it to the couple alone. But this use, as such, violates the essential order of man in himself, both as an *individual* and as a *member of the human race*."[10] In every individual, he explains, reason should rule over passion; but it does not when spouses perform in a self-centered way "an act which is primarily an act *of the species*, to be performed by the spouses as representatives of the human species and acting in its behalf".[11] What, then, does the good of the species require? Maximum numbers in every family, so in every country, and on the Earth as a whole? Obviously not. And Vermeersch makes clear that such is not his meaning.[12] But in that case what does distinguish onanistic intercourse from unfruitful intercourse between sterile partners, say, or during infertile periods? Were maximum procreation obligatory, we could excuse the sterile, since they can do no better, and accuse the onanists, since they can. But as it is, what crucial difference distinguishes the one group from the other? Why does Vermeersch condemn the one and not the other? Well, he explains, in one case the manner is natural, in the other it is not.[13] That is, in one case the spouses actively impede procreation, in the other they don't.[14] However, we already knew that; it simply spells out the meaning of the terms used to designate the groups. And supposedly Vermeersch is not proposing a mere moral tautology. He is not saying: "Onanism is wrong because it is onanism." Yet he offers no further clarification of his reasons and therefore of his meaning. The trail just disappears.

5. More complex is the teaching of St. Thomas which I shall now consider, in preparation for later study of the Council of Vienne. Several decades before the Council's declaration concerning the soul as form of the body, St. Thomas expressed himself in terms like these:

> Should anyone wish to maintain that the intellective soul is not the form of the body, he would have to find some way of making the act of understanding an act of this particular person. For each is conscious that it is he himself that understands.[15]

A friend of mine once expostulated about a third party who "didn't even know what a formal cause was". I held my peace. Some months later he raised the subject again. "You know, this notion of formal causality is more problematic than I supposed." St. Thomas seems never to have had any misgivings about the meaningfulness of his doctrine,[16] nor have his commentators seriously questioned it.[17] Thus they have not provided the sort of explanations which might have genuinely clarified his teaching or have established a sense for words such as those I have just quoted. I, at least, have never succeeded in finding a coherent interpretation.

A familiar illustration, dating from Aristotle,[18] compares matter and form in a substance with material and shape in a statue (for instance bronze in the shape of Jupiter). Shape is, of course, an accidental form, and is perceptible, whereas a substantial form is neither. Furthermore, there is no intrinsic resemblance between the two kinds of form. "Rather it is because the *relation* between the shape and the bronze in man-made objects resembles the relation between substantial form and matter in natural objects, that this illustration is employed, so as to explain the unknown through the well known."[19] Similarly, "that which is related to natural substances as bronze is related to a statue or wood to a bed . . . we call *prime matter*."[20]

As an explanation, this is inadequate. For if an accidental form such as shape differs so greatly from a substantial form, and if wood or bronze differs so notably from prime matter, it is hardly likely, *a priori*, that the relation between prime matter and substantial form is *just* the same as that between material and shape. We may legitimately suppose, therefore, that St. Thomas viewed the relation between matter and form as *somewhat* similar to that between material and shape. But in what respect? If the two components of substantial composition are in themselves as yet unknown and uncomprehended, and by all indications extremely different from the things we do know, how are we to discern the point of the comparison? To grasp the difficulty more concretely, consider a case like the following. If I know the relation between color and shape in an object, and you tell me that pitch and timbre are similarly related in a note, I may then surmise your meaning. You are alluding, perhaps, to facts like the following: timbre and pitch are simultaneous, as color and shape are; pitch is as inseparable from timbre as color is from shape; timbre and pitch, like color and shape, are just two traits of a more comprehensive whole (the note also has volume, for instance, as the object has weight). But you are not alluding, say, to the fact that color fills the shape, or to the fact that shape is revealed by differences in color. The analogy does not extend that far. But suppose, now, that you do not identify the terms of the comparable relationship, but merely call them A and B, and say that they are related somewhat as shape and color are in an object. In that case I shall not be able to specify the respects in which the analogy holds; I shall not know which of many possible points of comparison you are referring to. And my ignorance concerning the terms of the relation will be still more complete. Are they, perhaps, volume and pitch in a note? Or speed and direction in a movement? Or will and intellect in a person? Or person and procession in the Trinity? I have no idea what the related terms are. For in these and countless other cases there is some analogy with the stated relation.

This difficulty concerning the intelligibility of substantial forms is not removed by saying, for instance, that "the nature and power of the soul are discovered through its activities."[21] For one thing, as St. Thomas himself was wont to point out, it is not the soul that acts, but the person; it is he who eats, talks, thinks, works. For another thing, how are we to understand the relation between the soul's "power" and its "nature"? If the two terms are synonymous, then the soul is simply an efficient cause, and formal causality does not differ from efficient. If they are not synonymous, then what is left to fill out the soul's "nature" after we have subtracted the dynamic aspect? What are the various "faculties" of the soul save powers, and what remains once we put these powers in brackets? Where is the strictly formal element?

Casting about for possible sources of understanding, we perhaps recall that in the Thomistic system "form is nothing but the act of matter."[22] Thus either the general doctrine of act and potency, or the correlative notion of prime matter, may serve as a guide to understanding. However, as Sertillanges has observed, the general doctrine of act and potency is to be understood from its instances, matter and form, and in particular from prime matter and substantial form, not vice versa.[23] And as for the second possibility, St. Thomas himself declared: "Since form does not exist for the sake of matter but rather matter for the sake of form, the form explains the character of the matter, not the other way round."[24] Perhaps the term "character" should be understood in a somewhat different sense than the one that interests us; but it is clear, in any case, that there is little likelihood of reciprocal clarification between these two terms, matter and form, or between any pair so intimately related. Thus (to cite simpler cases) if the notion "faster" or "above" is incomprehensible to me, there is small chance that I shall understand the concept "slower" or "below" any better. If rights are a mystery to me, I shall not be enlightened by a definition in terms of obligations. And so on. And even were the link between matter and form more clearly conceived at one end than at the other, it is evident which end that would be. "Matter is not a principle of knowledge," wrote St. Thomas, "nor does it determine anything in a genus or species."[25]

But form does. And there may lie the missing lead. "Notice," St. Thomas reminds us, "that form pins matter down to a determinate kind of thing, rather as a supplementary property shapes a substance of a species to a determinate mode of being, as a human being is limited by being white."[26] Thus substantial forms are essential forms; together with prime matter, they constitute the essence. And once we discriminate essential properties from accidental, the basic intelligibility of substantial forms will stand revealed. But how is that discrimination to be performed?

The Platonic, Aristotelian, and Scholastic approach to essences, natures, and forms is, I think, aptly summed up by Wittgenstein's comparison: in order to find the real artichoke, we divest it of its leaves.[27] For no one leaf is the artichoke or essential to it. Thus the real artichoke seems to be hidden beneath the surface. Even if we never perceive it, we are sure it is there. For certainly there is an artichoke, and it is not these mere leaves. Thus for St. Thomas the form "is in itself unknown and becomes known through the accidents".[28] The human form, for instance, must not be confused with build, appearance, activities, or anything perceptible; for any such feature—leg, lung, smile, or all-night party—might be missing and the individual would still be a man, just as any one leaf might be removed and the artichoke would remain. So these leaves too must be stripped away.[29] But what is the quintessential artichoke (the essence, or the form) we seek? Is the doctrine of the "real artichoke" intelligible? Is it not rather a muddle expressed in intelligible-sounding words?

I shall not follow scholastic reasoning through all possible twists and turns. It is unrealistic to suppose that a vast, interlocking, highly speculative doctrine such as hylemorphism, proposed by thinkers of the stature of Aristotle and Aquinas, can be disposed of in the course of two or three pages. At most I can suggest the plausibility of my position and make the reader aware that there is a genuine problem where he perhaps perceived none. And I can illustrate, by means of these few remarks on formal causality, a typical pattern which difficulties tend to take when one looks into the meaning of obscure metaphysical theories.

The terminology and the arguments suggest a variety of possibilities, but each possibility seems to be negated by some other element in the doctrine, so that to accept the explanation is to end in contradiction and to reject it is to be left empty-handed. "Either emptiness or incoherence" seems to be the unacceptable verdict for the doctrine as a whole. Thus, in the present instance, if we follow up the lead suggested by the word "form" we are likely to suppose that the form of a thing consists in its peculiar organization, of tissues, organs, members, and so on. But of course a thing's structure is perceptible and the form, we are told, is not. If, then, we have recourse to causal reasoning and pass from perceived effects to the unperceived cause, the term of the inference is an efficient cause, whereas the causality to be explained is "formal". If we gratuitously suppose that there must be something common to all members of a class, for instance to human beings, and that this hidden something is the essence (or the essential form, according to the context) which makes a man a man, we arrive at the conclusion that the term "man" is applied according to a criterion hidden from all those who use it. It is because of their common humanity, we are told, that we predicate the term of all human individuals; yet this identical humanity is not only imperceptible but inconceivable. It is the artichoke that has no leaves, the one hidden inside.

For present purposes of illustration, these remarks may suffice. The pattern I have described, of alternative interpretations each cancelled in turn, is certainly found elsewhere if not here. However, in the next chapter I shall need to have been right about this particular case. And so long as I have not thoroughly explored all possibilities, the reader may feel that my point is not established. Five dead-ends do not prove an impasse. So I would point out that no matter how successful some untried line of interpretation may turn out to be, St. Thomas's doctrine of substantial forms cannot be dissociated from his teaching on essences, nor can the latter be understood apart from what he says about definition. ("Properly speaking, the essence is what is expressed by the definition.")[30] And concerning definition, he, like so many others before and after him, fell into confusion of a kind I shall now illustrate in the case of William James.

6. James's definition of truth is well known:

> This thesis is what I have to defend. The truth of an idea is not a stagnant property inherent in it. Truth *happens* to an idea. It *becomes* true, is *made* true by events. Its verity *is* in fact an event, a process: the process namely of its verifying itself, its veri-*fication*. Its validity is the process of its valid-*ation*." "Such is the large loose way in which the pragmatist interprets the word agreement. He treats it altogether practically. He lets it cover any process of conduction from a present idea to a future terminus, provided only it run prosperously."[31]

I have chosen this sampling to illustrate a more profound form of incoherence, characterized by conflict not merely between concept and concept within uniformly factual or conceptual discourse, but between alternative forms of discourse. There is a clash of language-games, and not just of terms. For consider the following basically diverse interpretations of James's intentions when he declared that truth is a process.

1. *Conceptual Interpretation:* In this account, James would be reporting the established meaning of the word "truth", determined by the contingent way in which English-speakers actually employ it. But were this his intention, he would have to rest his case on usage, so cite and analyze typical utterances in which the word "truth" occurs. And this he did not even attempt. We seem entitled to conclude, therefore, that he did not envisage his theory as a report of the word's established meaning. He was not doing semantics.

2. *Personal Definition:* It seems still more evident that he did not intend to propose a new meaning, a personal definition, in place of the existing one. For declarations about what truth *is* hardly suggest such an aim, and it would have required James to compare his definition with an existing meaning, demonstrate the pragmatic advantages of the proposed terminology, and so on. That is, discussion would have taken a very different tack from that actually pursued.

3. *Factual Interpretation:* According to this reading, James would be proposing an alternative description of truth, not a different meaning for the word "truth". He and his opponents would both be referring to the same thing, truth, but would be ascribing different properties to it. But James himself ruled out this interpretation. He said flatly that he was *not* talking about any static property such as his adversaries proposed, but about a process. And surely there is no one referent described by James as a process and by rationalists as a static state of correspondence. The disputants were not giving different descriptions of one thing, therefore, but talking about different things. They were not using the word "truth" in the same sense, did not give it the same meaning. Accordingly, they were not contradicting one another, or offering alternative statements of

fact. If one person says "John is tall" and another says "John is short," and, on further inquiry, it turns out that they are referring to different individuals, their statements are not contradictory.

But they are factual. So may not James's assertion have been? May not both he and his opponents have been right, and both have been stating facts? Well, what fact did James state? What did he add to the description of the process when he said the process is truth? What more do we learn about the process in virtue of this statement? Nothing. When a person points to a man and says, "This is John," no description is given. Likewise, when someone points to a color and says, "This is red," he does not describe the color. And when James picks out verbally the reference of his appellation, then says, "This is truth," he too gives no description. He attaches a label. A description is possible only in virtue of an agreed meaning for the terms used, and James and his interlocutors had reached no such agreement.

4. *Value Interpretation:* The interpretation of James's statement as a veiled commendation of his preferred values is no more promising, but should be considered; for values, not facts, dictated his answer, and the principal outcome of his teaching is a shift of values. "The whole function of philosophy," James declared, "ought to be to find out what definite difference it will make to you and me, at definite instants of our life, if this world-formula or that world-formula be the true one."[32] This is straight-forward, undisguised value talk, and is based on corresponding pragmatic arguments, for instance: "It is astonishing to see how many philosophical disputes collapse into insignificance the moment you subject them to this simple test of tracing a concrete consequence."[33] However, James does not use such arguments to show that truth is a process that goes prosperously. He could hardly do so and still maintain that he was advancing a "theory". Clearly, James did not regard his proposal as simply a disguised recommendation, nor does the average reader. He does not translate James's "Truth is a

process" into "Look to the consequences," even though James's words heighten his interest in consequences, and were intended to.

5. *Pragmatist Interpretation:* A thinker should be taken on his own terms. Now James became a pragmatist through accepting C. S. Peirce's definition of meaning, and his treatment of truth (it might be suggested) follows logically from that acceptance. Peirce asserted quite generally "that the *total* meaning of the predication of an intellectual concept is contained in an affirmation that, under all conceivable circumstances of a given kind . . . the subject of the predication would behave in a certain general way. . . ."[34] Since "true" is such an intellectual concept, James looked for the consequences of an idea's being true rather than false, saw that true ideas lead to success whereas false ideas lead to failure, and concluded that this result—this process of successful leading—is the meaning of the word "true". He was simply giving a Peircian meaning.

Though this interpretation sounds more plausible as an account James himself might give, it too fails to clarify the situation, for: (a) Peirce's own procedure in defining meaning leaves us in the dark in the same way, concerning the preceding alternatives; (b) accordingly no clear consequences follow from it; it is not at all clear, for instance, whether the alleged identity between the consequences of being true and the meaning of "true" entitles us to conclude that the consequences *are* truth. If, for instance, someone were to insist that the whole "meaning" of pearl-diving is the finding of pearls, would we be entitled to conclude that pearl-diving *is* finding pearls? There seems only one conclusion: James was in a muddle, and his doctrine is unintelligible.

An overall pattern can be detected in this example, one typical of innumerable cases. Philosophers, theologians, and others have shown special predilection for questions of the form "What is X?", where "X" is a single term ("truth", "beauty", etc.). But they have seldom understood or explained to others just what game they were playing, according to what rules, on the basis of what suppositions, in view of what expectations. Lovejoy pinpoints one principal confusion when he warns: "There is nothing about which it is more essential that a philosopher should, from the start of any inquiry or discussion, be absolutely clear in his own mind, and make himself clear to his readers, than the discrimination of his definitions from his assertions; for this discrimination is the prime requisite for the avoidance of purely verbal issues and controversies."[35] Furthermore, not only should he distinguish concept from fact; he must keep value distinct from both. Yet a typical situation is the one exemplified in James's treatment of truth. Time and again, the conceptual, the factual, and the evaluative become inextricably entangled, in the following manner: a philosopher who knows how to use a key word like "truth" yet has little reflective understanding of the concept does not suppose for a moment that his problem lies in language, so states his question in objective, factual-sounding terms. He does not ask, "What is the meaning of the word 'X'?", or, "How do we use the word 'X'?", but, "What is X?" Ignoring the linguistic parameter, therefore, which alone could guide him to a legitimate answer, and having no clear idea what he seeks or why, he is guided more by preferences than by reasons and ends up conferring the honorific title ("truth", "meaning", "beauty", "reality", etc.) on his favorite. Where the intellect provides no guidance the will takes command, and value preferences dictate the answer.

In the next chapter I shall have more to say about the reasons and relevance of James's failure. And I shall attend, more fully than at the end of Chapter Two, to the sort of misgivings the reader may have felt as I ran through the opinions of Vermeersch, St. Thomas and James, and consigned them to semantic limbo. In one case or the other, wouldn't it be possible, with good will and a little ingenuity, to arrange the data differently and thereby reach a favorable decision? Though plausible, my verdict may have seemed too clear, the arguments too neat. Here I shall only say in reply that my brief accounts are not proposed as faithful representations of the whole complex situation, but as an ordered, suggestive, reasonably quick way of presenting my genuine puzzlement with regard to this basic question: If I were asked to pass judgment on the doctrine in question, what would I be agreeing or disagreeing with? *What would be true, what false?* What, for instance, would I be asserting if I agreed with Vermeersch that spouses act "as representatives of the human species" and that artificial contraception therefore "violates the essential order of man in himself"? I have no idea. I find myself in a similar quandary concerning St. Thomas's doctrine of forms: what would I be affirming if I acknowledged its truth? How, too, are we to agree or disagree with James, so long as we do not know whether his claim is conceptual or factual, and whether it is a claim at all and not a veiled proposal or panegyric? In each of these cases I cannot discover enough consistent evidence to justify any one option as *the* correct interpretation.

It is now time to consider whether there are or can be such statements among the Church's teachings and whether we should, therefore, make room for a third category in our consideration of magisterial pronouncements: true, false, and *truthless*.

CHAPTER FIVE

Is Saul Too
Among the Prophets?

Some of the best minds have fallen, unawares, into incoherence or have failed to provide meaning for their words. It is to be expected, therefore, that the statements of churchmen—popes, bishops, and theologians—should sometimes reveal a similar lack. Only a special providence could prevent it, and there seems no solid reason to suppose such intervention, at least of a general sort that might assure us in advance that all magisterial statements are certainly meaningful. Such is the conclusion of the present chapter, and such the general line of reasoning; I consider first the natural probability that some magisterial statements lack meaning, then the improbability that meaning is divinely assured.

To some, I may seem to be attacking the magisterium. But I am simply giving what appears to me the obviously correct answer to an important but neglected question, in the conviction that the Church cannot be hurt by a disinterested search for the truth, whereas she could be disastrously harmed by the notion that "pastoral" considerations take precedence over the truth.

Truth is the criterion of the Church's genuine good, not her supposed good the criterion of truth, or of the truth which it is safe to divulge.

As I pointed out at the start, the question I am discussing parallels the question of infallibility, and that question has been *asked* concerning all Church teaching. With regard to magisterial statements in general, the answer is that they may sometimes be false. But with regard to specific categories of statements, satisfying certain conditions, the possibility of falsehood has been ruled out. In my treatment, I shall ask whether all magisterial statements, without distinction, have meaning; but I shall not go on to the further question, whether the meaningfulness of certain categories is assured. This may appear a serious omission. After all, if on occasion magisterial statements may even be false, isn't it evident that they may sometimes lack meaning? What we need to know, it might be urged, is whether statements of a specific category—in particular *ex cathedra* pronouncements—invariably make sense. However, this is not a typical reaction. And I have reason to believe that even asking the more specific question would be regarded as a threat, rather than as a serious search for the truth in a new area of inquiry. So I shall leave the focus wide. My question throughout shall be: Is the meaningfulness of magisterial statements guaranteed by the fact that they are magisterial statements?

The sense of this question is, I hope, clear by now—clear in its very lack of clarity. In Chapters One and Three I explained why I place little faith in definitions. Still, at the end of Chapter Two, relying on the preceding series of examples to clarify and justify the suggestion, I proposed to extend the term "meaningless" to statements which are even covertly incoherent. This application of the word has now been illustrated by further samples, in the second half of Chapter Four. When I speak of ultimate incoherence, I have in mind the sort of situation revealed by the analyses of St. Thomas's doctrine of forms and James's theory of truth. Such models provide more clarity

than would even a precise-sounding definition; for any definition must be explained in the long run by reference to just such
sample cases, as many and as varied as possible. And even
after such concrete reference, one must conclude the explanation by saying: "You now see the kind of thing I mean. But
cases will undoubtedly be encountered which do not closely
conform to any of these models. You must treat them accordingly, taking both the similarities and dissimilarities into account, and seeing whether your conclusions still hold." Avoidance of the easy way of general definitions and abstract
principles, with their illusory clarity, is good preparation for
that close attention to detail which is indispensable in studying
any individual statement of the magisterium.

The important thing is that the reader should understand
what I am talking about, not that he should accept my use of
the words "meaning" and "meaningless". But I fear that some
may react as follows: "The conclusion reached rests on your
notion of meaning. Change the definition of meaning and the
conclusion about magisterial statements alters. And I suspect
that the definition should be changed. For isn't it rather farfetched to suppose that the solemn declaration of some pope or
council may be meaningless?" One answer to such misgivings
has already been suggested: from the proof itself, learn what is
proved. The very examples examined, I said, would illustrate
further the sense of my thesis that magisterial pronouncements
may be meaningless; and such a thesis, if established, retains its
significance regardless of what one thinks about the definition.
(Point out to a homeowner that termites are gnawing his
rafters, and he will be little concerned if you slip and call them
ants.)

Another reply would be to suggest that a reader who feels
these doubts should clarify in his own mind what he takes
meaning to be. If he does not know what answer to give, he
may rest assured that his misgivings have no solid reflective
basis. If he is ready with an answer, one which applies to
complex theological doctrines, I would then suggest that he

consider what guarantee there is that all magisterial statements possess meaning as he has defined it. Any definition which makes their meaningfulness appear unproblematic is certainly a gross simplification both of the concept "meaning" and of the facts of language.

There is one popular model, I know, which requires only that the words express a thought, where "thought" means "mental representation". Then even if the words are unfortunately vague, or one proposition conflicts with another, each individual statement retains a sense. For the person who writes or utters it certainly thinks something, and whatever thought the words express is their meaning. In this view, to claim that a magisterial statement is meaningless would be equivalent to saying that its author or authors merely set pen to paper, without a thought in their heads. And that surely is absurd.

Yes, but so is this conception of language. For if representation in the mind of the speaker were the necessary and sufficient condition for meaningful sentences, it would follow that any series of sounds uttered by a thinking person would automatically be meaningful. If, for instance, someone said "Walla walla woo," while thinking about the weather or the stock exchange, the words would be a statement about the weather or the stock exchange. It will be objected, no doubt, that those who hear the utterance do not think about the weather or the stock exchange, and that is why the sounds are meaningless. They fail to communicate the speaker's thought to others. This answer is still very far from the truth, but close enough for present purposes. For the reader must surely realize how dubious it is with regard to many theological and magisterial statements (or any statements whatever, for that matter) whether the same mental representations occur in the minds of those who read them as occurred in the minds of their authors. Even such a simplified criterion makes the meaningfulness of magisterial statements problematic enough so that the reader should no longer be tempted, if he ever was, to consider the thesis of this chapter farfetched.

Language, said the later Wittgenstein, is not a mental calculus, but a form of life. "We talk, we utter words, and only *later* get a picture of their life."[1] So it may happen that we, looking back from the vantage point of several centuries and with the detachment of spectators, can now perceive that thinkers have sometimes wandered into well-concealed labyrinths, and stumbled about aimlessly, until they hit on an exit and continued on their way. Consider the simile in detail. Just as someone might insist that any magisterial statement certainly says *something*, so too someone might argue that a man in a maze is surely going somewhere; for he is moving. But in another ordinary sense of the words, he is not going anywhere; he is lost. And the same may be said of a person wandering in the labyrinth of language. In the corresponding, theologically more important sense of the expression "say something", his statements may say nothing at all. If we look at just isolated phrases, their incoherence or lack of meaning is not evident, just as a person's movements along a single lane of a maze may look sure and purposeful if we pay no attention to his previous and subsequent movements. Both *could* form part of a coherent whole. To estimate the true situation, therefore, we must take a wider view. And this is often difficult. For we may have lost our way in the same maze.

A second objection against the proposed inquiry may arise from recent emphasis on the Church as the true subject of teaching authority. It is because the powers of darkness will not prevail against Christ's Church that they cannot prevail against Peter in any way that would entail her ruin. So why am I focusing on the magisterium rather than on the faith of the whole flock? My main answer is the same as before: I am using the Wittgensteinian technique of simple language-games. In comparison with a single, precisely worded statement of a pope or council, the faith of the whole Church is vast, vague, and unmanageable. A magisterial pronouncement, though far more complex than the simple examples with which I began, is itself a relatively simple sample in comparison with Christian belief in general on the topic of the pronouncement. To paraphrase Wittgenstein: when we look at such formulations of the magisterium, the mist dissipates, and we are able to make clear-cut distinctions and ask pointed questions which then turn out to be relevant for other cases as well. In fact, all the more important conclusions of the present chapter can be extended to the faith of the Church as a whole. And of course the magisterium has great importance in, if not for, itself.

Yet I do not wish to exaggerate the significance of the conclusions I shall reach about meaning. Often a theologian is interested in the meaning of a statement only insofar as it reveals the belief of the writer. And it is conceivable that a meaningless statement should do that almost as effectively as a meaningful one. As a simple illustration, consider the professor's statement in Chapter Two (#9) that he had $\sqrt[3]{383}$ friends, and suppose now that he was in earnest. Since the cube of seven is 343, and 383 is both a similar number and closer to that cube than to any other, we might reasonably infer a lapse of memory or slip of the tongue and conclude that the professor believed and meant to say that he had seven friends. His failure to say it would not then be a failure to convey it, if we had the wits to decipher *his* intention, *his* meaning, as distinct from the statement's. These three—a speaker's intention, his meaning, and the meaning of his statement—are closely related but should not be confused. The only one I am directly interested in is the third.

The Likelihood of Meaningless Magisterial Statements

The verdict which I propose as the correct one, that the meaningfulness of magisterial statements is not guaranteed, will be argued in two stages, one *a priori*, the other *a posteriori*. Language, I shall suggest in the *a priori* part, is such that we should expect even intelligent people to get lost in it, especially when they are theorizing; and in fact philosophers, even analytic ones, have so often fallen into meaningless incoherence that it would be a miracle if theologians did not follow suit. For, if anything, the danger is greater in theology than in philosophy. The *a posteriori* part of the argument will consist in case studies of magisterial statements which seem to bear out this contention. Their apparent lack of meaning is a further strong argument for actual lack in these or similar cases. Though unable, for reasons of space and the very logic of the inquiry, to definitely establish the absence of coherent sense in even a single case, I may claim, nonetheless, to have at least demonstrated the great plausibility of my thesis.

A theologian might expect that somewhere in the course of the discussion I would employ a more direct approach. In fact he may already be puzzled by my failure to mention theological sources and what they have to say on the question. But if he reflects for a moment, he should realize how little Scripture and tradition say directly on the matter I am treating. Some magisterial documents touch on questions of meaning, but they do not treat the radical question of meaningfulness. As for the implicit beliefs revealed by more explicit teachings, it is clear that the authors of encyclicals and decrees, like those who read them, have supposed they all made sense from start to finish; but this unreflective conviction can hardly be accepted unquestioningly as a matter of faith. After all, the authors of magisterial statements consistently supposed them to be true as well as meaningful, but nobody would claim on that account that all were true. So I must take the approach I have described and work out an answer on my own.

1. The A Priori Approach

Our great ignorance of how language works has two principal explanations: first, the great variety and complexity of language; second, the unreflective way in which we employ it. The former corresponds to the number and variety of the occasions on which we use words, the purposes to which we put them, the activities into which we integrate them. But these are innumerable. Language pervades the whole of our lives, characterizing every phase of human activity—religious, social, artistic, economic, scientific, academic, recreational, and so on. Even our silent prayers or reflections are conducted in words. No one who has not attentively explored this vast continent of verbal symbolism can have an accurate notion of its geography. But in the course of speech we are not attentive to words, and cannot be. To serve as a medium, language must remain transparent. Communication would break down if we had to constantly reflect not only on what to say but on how to say it, and not only on what others say but how they say it. It is no accident, therefore, nor a disgrace to human intelligence, if we know so well how to use words but so imperfectly how we use them.

Reflective knowledge of language becomes necessary when we move from everyday affairs to speculative discourse. There, for instance in philosophy and theology, to be ignorant of language and its requirements is to run the risk of no longer speaking intelligibly. Or rather, it is to be doomed from the start. There are two reasons for this: first, the speculative thinker is a linguistic pioneer and, second, the areas of his research are heavily linguistic. Let us consider each of these points.

When discussing ordinary matters in ordinary ways and in ordinary circumstances, we follow well-trodden linguistic paths without any fear of going astray. We may be mistaken about the matters we discuss, but we are not generally mistaken in the way we discuss them. We may err factually when we claim that our team will win or that the other driver was at fault, but not linguistically; we are not talking nonsense. The speculative thinker, on the other hand, ventures into new territory, asking unusual questions about unusual topics with small help from familiar contexts which might give clear sense to his words. And he repeatedly complicates his task by introducing a whole new conceptual apparatus, systematically altering familiar terms, often without realizing how extensive his innovations are. Thus he strikes out into a linguistic wilderness in which he may easily lose his way and where, in any case, he will have to hack his own path. If he does not notice that he has left the road, he will certainly lose his way. Or rather, he already has.

Furthermore, the field of his inquiries is not that of the scientist, historian, sociologist, psychologist, or the like. The world of symbolism more than the world of nature is the realm in which he needs to find his way. Time and again, conceptual unclarity motivates his search, unclarity which can only be removed, therefore, by reflection on his conceptual system, that is, on language. His frequent failure to grasp the conceptual nature of his problems and to recognize the identity between conceptual inquiries and linguistic inquiries is itself part of the unclarity to be remedied.

A concrete case—for instance James's treatment of truth, studied in the previous chapter (#6)—may make these vague and general remarks more pointed and convincing. "What is truth?", James asked, and did not realize how problematic his question was, for it sounded just like many we ask every day. Someone hears the word "isomorphism" for the first time and asks, "What is isomorphism?" The person who used the word replies with a definition, precise or approximate, not with a theory. For it is clear from the circumstances what the other person needs and what sort of answer he expects. He is not asking for anything hidden or difficult or controversial, but for the meaning known to everyone who uses the word. In James's case, however, the situation was entirely different. He presupposed familiarity with the word and with all such common examples as might be used in explaining its meaning. In the sense in which some people know the meaning of "isomorphism" we all know the meaning of "truth". What, then, did James lack? What was the point of his question? It was incumbent on him, as author of the question, to indicate its sense, for everyday usage did not. Thus from the very start of his inquiry a philosopher must be aware of language. For it is there, in the question itself, that he often loses his way. He does not even notice that he has left the beaten path.

Next, notice that in reflecting on the sense of his question about truth, James could not have adequately listed the alternatives without making the basic distinction between a verbal, conceptual question and a non-verbal, non-conceptual question, and between different sorts of conceptual queries. He would have had to envisage the possibility that a question which makes no explicit mention of meaning or of words may nevertheless be an inquiry about the meaning of words. And he would have had to realize the difference between a question about the meaning of a word and a question about its reference. That is, he would have had to know his way around in language, to an extent few philosophers (or theologians) have.

Furthermore, with regard to both of the main alternatives—the conceptual and the non-conceptual—major linguistic considerations would have had to be noticed and kept in mind throughout the ensuing inquiry. When the question is one about meaning, it is necessary to determine whether the actual meaning is to be reported, on the basis of linguistic evidence, or a new meaning is to be advanced, for pragmatic reasons. When the question is about the reference—for instance when it is about truth and not about the meaning of "truth"—the relation to the word must nevertheless guide the whole procedure. For either the things to be studied are all those to which the term is actually applied, in which case a linguistic inquiry into its application is necessary, or a more narrow sampling is in view, so must be more precisely designated than by the mere term "X" in the formula "What is X?" The philosopher is on his own and can take nothing for granted. He *must* pay attention to words.

Finally, notice the particular term James considered so important: "truth". Many would call it a semantic expression, but he did not. For truth, he said, is first and foremost a property of our ideas or beliefs. Just look in the dictionary! Yet when I looked in quite a large dictionary I found no mention of beliefs, one mention of ideas, and many references to propositions and statements. The primary sense of "true" is, in fact, linguistic. A belief is true if the proposition which expresses it is true; and the proposition is true if each of the words is used in conformity with its overall use in the language. Repeatedly a key concept which is thought to be psychological turns out to be largely or primarily linguistic. Thus linguistic reflection on the sense of the initial question may lead to an investigation which is linguistic to the second power: the linguistic study of a linguistic concept.

In endless ways, philosophical inquiry requires that a person not only pay attention to language but be well prepared through long reflection on it to note when and how the linguistic dimension is relevant, perhaps crucial. The trouble is that only someone with considerable linguistic awareness notices the necessity, for, as I pointed out at the start, the use of signs is so complex and so unreflective an activity that most people are not only ignorant of language but ignorant of their own ignorance. "Man possesses the ability to construct languages capable of expressing every sense, without having any idea how each word has meaning or what its meaning is—just as people speak without knowing how the individual sounds are produced."[2]

The results are what one might expect. Few of the world's great philosophers have made consistent sense. For few have been sufficiently aware of the linguistic medium they all employed. To substantiate this claim, which may well sound brash if left general and vague, let us consider again James's treatment of truth. The question "What is truth?" belongs to an extremely common species. Since the days of Socrates and before, endless philosophers have asked questions of the form "What is X?", where X is knowledge, or beauty, or justice, or life, or goodness, or meaning, etc., etc. Yet how many have seen the necessity of clarifying the question's sense? How many have made the distinctions or asked the basic questions I raised with regard to James's inquiry into truth? How many have gotten as far as the first and most important distinction, between the conceptual and the non-conceptual? Not only James's question, but his procedure is typical. So too, therefore, is the ultimate incoherence of his "theory". And this is but one illustration from among many.

Analytic philosophers have not fared much better in this respect than others. Consider for instance Wittgenstein's later verdict[3] that his own *Tractatus Logico-Philosophicus* is ultimately incoherent and meaningless. Though the *Tractatus* is an important and influential work, by the most capable linguistic philosopher of this or any other century, this severe judgment can be verified in point after point. But if it is thus in the green wood, what in the dry? Most philosophers have paid much less attention to language than have linguistic philosophers; few of the latter have stressed as strongly as Wittgenstein the power of language to confuse and mislead us; no other, I would say, has demonstrated equal penetration in the study of language; yet he ended up writing in the margin of his youthful classic: "Every one of these sentences is the expression of an illness."[4] Though architectonically beautiful and exceptionally consistent, the whole work is ultimately incoherent. Repeatedly, if asked to agree or disagree with the *Tractatus*, we must reply with the later Wittgenstein: "It depends on how you understand the words; I don't know yet what they mean."[5]

It might seem, though, from my earlier remarks in Chapter Four, that there is less danger in theology and less need of analytic skill. The meaningfulness of revealed truths, I suggested, is guaranteed by their origin and need not be established by the theologian, whereas it is incumbent on the philosopher to clarify whatever is unclear in his statements. However, even within this traditional perspective, which many theologians question, of a transcendent revelation through Christ completed in apostolic times, serious problems of meaning remain. For the statements of Christ contained in the gospels are not his exact words. They have at least been through the complex process of translation. And as the years pass, the revelation gets interpreted, synthesized, theorized. Thus a thorny problem arises for any theologian concerned with the problem of meaningfulness. Were the propositions of Scripture, Fathers, councils, or popes merely human theories, the theologian could be as demanding as towards any scientific hypothesis or philosophical doctrine; he could ask or search for an explanation. On the other hand, were the propositions all synonymous with words from the mouth of Christ and he regarded in the traditional manner as one who spoke with clear, transcendent knowledge of what he said, the theologian could welcome them without qualms about their meaningfulness. Finally, as a third possibility, were it possible at least to sort out analytically the human from the divine, he could then adopt each attitude in turn, that of the man from Missouri towards the human accretions, that of the docile believer, the man born blind, the child who hears his parents say incomprehensible things, towards the directly revealed content. But none of these alternatives is verified. So what is the theologian to do?

This question is not an easy one to answer. Nor is the answer easy to apply. But theologians, in general untroubled about meaningfulness, have not usually noticed there was any problem. And there are other difficulties of the same sort which they have equally neglected, for instance with regard to the methodological implications of analogy. So what are the chances that, so often flying blind and without instruments, they have avoided mishaps? Having special problems of their own concerning meaning, over and above those common to philosophy and theology, but frequently lacking the philosopher's analytic training, what are the chances that they have fared better than he? Isn't it quite possible that they have done worse, not only than Wittgenstein, but than less talented linguistic philosophers, or even than non-linguistic philosophers? And isn't it unlikely, therefore, that down through the ages magisterial statements have always made impeccable sense? When so many of those who formulated them were incapable of adequate linguistic reflection, isn't it patently unlikely that all their utterances, on such abstruse matters, should stand up under the sort of scrutiny to which Wittgenstein subjected his analytic masterpiece? It would certainly be no disgrace to their authors or the Church, if some of them revealed the familiar traces of our common fallibility. This should be kept in mind as I now proceed to examine actual statements of the magisterium. If they fall, they fall to the human level—to the level of Plato, Russell, Hegel, or Wittgenstein—not to that of the village idiot.

2. The A Posteriori Approach

Since a full treatment of any magisterial statement would occupy at least a chapter and probably a full book, I shall confine myself to two. My aim is not to establish beyond the shadow of a doubt that each of these statements is ultimately unintelligible, but to suggest how plausible the suggestion is, and thereby indicate the still greater probability that some such statements, if not these precise ones, fail to pass muster. A factual slip on my part or an oversight in the argument may save one or the other; but can all kindred statements be rescued in similar fashion? There are many others about which similar doubts may be had; I did not have to hunt for these two examples.

(a) Of all magisterial pronouncements about the soul, the most famous, the most frequently repeated in the magisterium, and the most frequently referred to and discussed, is this passage from the Council of Vienne:

Furthermore, with the approval of the sacred council mentioned previously, We condemn as erroneous and opposed to Catholic truth every doctrine and opinion that rashly asserts that the substance of the rational, intellectual soul

is not truly and by its own nature the form of the human
body, or that casts doubt on this matter. And we define
that, whoever presumes to assert, defend, or stubbornly
hold that the rational or intellectual soul is not of its own
nature and essentially the form of the body, is to be considered a heretic.[6]

(Porro doctrinam omnem seu positionem temere asseren-
tem, aut vertentem in dubium, quod substantia animae rationalis seu intellectivae vere ac per se humani corporis
non sit forma, velut erroneam ac veritati catholicae inimi-
cam fidei, praedicto sacro approbante Concilio reproba-
mus: definientes . . . quod quisquis deinceps asserere, de-
fendere seu tenere pertinaciter praesumpserit, quod anima
rationalis seu intellectiva non sit forma corporis humani
per se et essentialiter, tanquam hereticus sit censendus.)
(DS 902)

Though I have never seen anyone question that these words
have some meaning, there has been much discussion and much
disagreement about what their meaning is.[7] And for anyone
alert to the more fundamental question, this fact is already
highly significant. A document which leaves its readers so completely in the dark may well be unintelligible. For intelligibility
is to be judged in relation to human readers, not angelic. However, commentators often bring confusion on themselves; so we
cannot judge automatically from the disparity of their explanations that the text itself is radically ambiguous.

Three main trends may be distinguished: one explanation
tends to void the Council's statement of philosophical content,
another reads it in the light of the general scholastic doctrine
current at that time, and a third interprets it in reference to one
particular Scholastic, Peter John Olivi, whom the Council had
specially in mind. A letter sent in the name of Pius IX tends in
the first direction. Decrees and definitions like those of Vienne,
it explains, impart only theological content, not philosophical

doctrine of a sort about which Catholics may legitimately disagree. The pronouncements of Vienne simply stress the substantial unity of human nature.[8] Bouillard exemplifies the second line of interpretation when he writes: "It is clear that the
Council is here using a technical notion and that it understands
it in the sense of the School at that time."[9] Jansen, whose
approach is in turn incompatible with both of these, declares:
"It is commonly acknowledged and assumed as a principle in
need of no further proof that the Council of Vienne wished to
condemn the error of Olivi and it alone. Hence according to all
the rules followed by anyone competent in questions concerning the history of dogma, the sense of the definition must be
determined from the historical circumstances and especially
from the heresy to which it is opposed; without a doubt, the
minute the doctrine of Olivi is established so is the sense of the
definition of the Council of Vienne."[10] As Schneider has re-
cently pointed out,[11] Jansen did not note sufficiently the possibility that the Council fathers did indeed desire to eliminate an
error they considered Olivi's, but were mistaken in judging it to
be his. So we may add a variant to the third approach and suggest that though the target was the one Jansen suggests, it was
not the genuine doctrine of the man whom, the Council, or at
least many of its members, meant to condemn. His *putative*
doctrine reveals the sense.

Each of these approaches has something to say for it: Pius's
as an indication of what the Council should have been doing
and of what people should expect of a council; Bouillard's as
an indication of the actual effect on the majority of those who
have read the conciliar statements; Jansen's (or the variant) as
an indication of what was on the fathers' minds and how they
conceived their task. So let us consider each approach in turn,
to see whether one or the other provides a plausible and coherent meaning for the text.

The wording of Pius's letter suggests that the philosophical
options envisaged and declared legitimate were simply different
brands of scholasticism more acceptable than Olivi's. That is,

the letter veers in the direction of Bouillard's reading. However, before passing to that alternative, let us consider what might be said in behalf of a truly open interpretation, compatible with any of the various philosophical positions, scholastic or non-scholastic, held by Catholics. Can it be plausibly argued that the Council of Vienne merely asserted the basic unity of man, which we all experience, without adding further specifications? Or does the soul in question have to be a hylemorphic form, and must its relation to the composite therefore be that of formal causality?

A good many readers, no doubt, knowing little or no scholastic philosophy, might receive only a vague, general impression that the Council wished to stress the unity of man. However, in this case the limitation on the content does not come from ignorance of fact (as when the average person learns nothing specific about the wave-lengths when he hears that an object is red), but from ignorance of the terminology. Putting the Council document in the hands of an untrained reader and judging the meaning from its effect on him would therefore be like judging the meaning of a work on nuclear physics from its effect on an uneducated reader. The only reasonable procedure is to consider the effect on those who know this jargon. For though we are all acquainted with words like "soul" and "form", the use the Council made of them is as remote from everyday use as is the scientific use of terms like "mass" and "momentum".

It might be suggested, in keeping with a common hermeneutic approach, that a statement's meaning should be judged from the meaning of the writer or speaker, and that the Council fathers, though they used precise-sounding scholastic terminology, may have meant merely to stress the unity of man. However, as I noted in Chapter One, a statement's meaning should not be too readily equated with the speaker's. And when, as is usually the case, a person does mean what his words mean, the words usually reveal his meaning more than his reveals theirs. There is in general no more important evidence for a person's meaning (whether as clue or criterion) than his words and their customary meanings. Thus very strong counter-evidence would have to be presented to show that a group of men trained in scholastic thought did not intend a scholastic meaning when they used scholastic terms. And to my knowledge no such evidence has ever been proposed with regard to the fathers at Vienne. So once again, the minimal reading appears implausible.

The second interpretation, in terms of general scholastic doctrine, encounters difficulties still more serious than those mentioned in my discussion of St. Thomas. For even if his hylemorphism were ultimately intelligible, it would not follow that there is an intelligible *scholastic* doctrine of hylemorphism. It is commonly said, I know, that the scholastics all agreed about matter and form but simply distributed them differently, some putting both in angels as well as in men while others insisted on the simplicity of angelic natures, some arguing for two or three souls in man and others for one, some teaching composition of matter and form in the soul itself while others rejected such composition, and so on. However, all this disagreement in doctrine reflects much diversity as well in the meaning of the terms; for the main criteria of sense in such abstract metaphysics, as in abstract mathematics, are precisely such moves as these. Accordingly, it may be urged, if the formulae of the Council of Vienne are to get their meaning from scholastic doctrine in general, they have no sense; for scholasticism used its hylemorphic terms in no single, consistent sense.

To grasp the situation more accurately, though, let us return to the simple paradigm "My car is red," and reflect that there too: (1) there is a disjunction of possibilities; and (2) the members of the disjunction are mutually incompatible. The car may be scarlet *or* rose, but it cannot be scarlet *and* rose all over. Similarly, we may suppose that the soul mentioned by Vienne is tripartite, bipartite, or single, that it is composed of spiritual matter and form or is noncomposite, and so on; but we cannot attribute to it all the conflicting properties proposed by various schools. This much, though, is no reason for complaint; practically any meaningful statement reveals a similar structure, for one constituent expression or for several. What, then, is the objection? How does the Council's statement, if interpreted in the way suggested by Bouillard, differ from these others?

The error to avoid here is the idea that just as one shade of red might verify the statement "My car is red," so one coherent form of hylemorphism could give meaning to the statement of Vienne. It would then appear that, since I have made no effort to show that *every* form is incoherent, my negative verdict is premature, to say the least. This mistaken impression comes from confusing meaning and truth. One member of a disjunction, though unknown, may *verify* a statement whose meaning rests on common knowledge of a variety of possibilities. But a single possibility, unknown or known to few, cannot establish any basis of *meaning* for a statement like that of Vienne. The various shades of red, people's acquaintance with them, their use of the word "red" to designate now one shade, now another —all these establish the meaning of the term "red", so that any statement which applies the predicate "red" to an object possessing one of these shades is automatically *true*, regardless of how many people know just what shade it is. All that is necessary is that the shade fall within the range of this common acquaintance and usage. But suppose now that among all the accounts of the soul as formal cause, or, more precisely, among those which preceded the Council of Vienne, there is one alone which is coherent, and that only its author and a few disciples both knew and accepted it, so perhaps learned something coherent when and if they read the Council's words. Does this supposition entitle us to say that such is the meaning of those words, or that they have a meaning? And if one were to stretch the word "meaning" that far, what importance would the question of meaning still have for realistic discussion of the Church's magisterium and the communication of truth? Instead of many genuine possibilities known to the whole population or a sizable proportion, there would be but a single possibility known to practically no one. And the privileged few would make sense of the Council's statements only if, *per accidens*, they were simple-minded enough to suppose that the Council was using the terms in the special sense accepted by that little-known school.

Thus, if it is true, as I have suggested, that St. Thomas's account of formal causality is not coherent, and if it is unlikely that the accounts of his contemporaries or predecessors are superior to his in this respect, and if in fact I have never encountered a coherent version antecedent to Vienne, I am not troubled by the possibility that somewhere in some forgotten volume an unsung genius straightened things out satisfactorily. A hidden gem may give truth to a statement but not meaning to a word, for instance to the word "form" when it appears in the decrees of Vienne—unless, perhaps, the fathers of the Council had that precise doctrine in view. We thus come to the third approach, that of Jansen.

As a solution to the problem of meaning, his approach, sharpening the focus, is perhaps the most promising; for if the system focused on reveals some sense, the Council document may itself make equal sense, by reflection. Furthermore, both the context and the wording of the decree do in fact suggest that it be read in relation to Olivi's teaching. His writings were the only ones in question, and were examined, attacked and defended at great length before the condemnatory decrees were formulated. It is reasonable to surmise, therefore, that in his statements we may discover the explanation of the Council's counter-statements.

Olivi never denied that the soul is the substantial form of the human body.[12] But, explains Jansen, he divided up the soul into three parts—the vegetative, the animal, and the rational—and had the rational part inform the body via the others, with which it was united by a common spiritual matter. The only direct relation he would admit between the body and the intellective part of the soul as such was one of governance. This apparent return of Plato's pilot in the boat was what worried the schoolmen and brought on Olivi's condemnation. It was not enough to admit that the soul was a substantial form and that the intellective part belonged to it. No, a rational part, if such there was, would have to inform the body *directly*, and *of itself!*[13]

But what does all this mean? True, as we follow such phrases we tend to illustrate them in our minds: each component—the spiritual matter, the intellective part of the soul, the animal part, the vegetative—has its own phantasmic representation, properly placed and appropriately linked by subtle mental movements whenever some verb requires a hook-up. But image-mongery is not understanding; it is just what we fall back on in an attempt to make sense of senseless words. Formal causality is problematic enough without distinguishing direct and indirect and dividing the soul into segments. I imagine that even many hylemorphists would recognize that such theories are hopelessly confused.[14] And any condemnation which derives its sense from them (I do not say merely: is motivated by them) is equally unintelligible. But that is the hypothesis we are considering.

The situation is as follows: Olivi's doctrine might fall under the Council's anathema either as a particular instance covered by a more general condemnation, or as the precise target of a general-sounding but equally definite denial. The first interpretation takes us back to the alternative already considered, of a general scholastic sense; the second lands us in the difficulty that the negative of a meaningless proposition is as meaningless as the affirmative (e.g., the denial that parsnips purr whenever they're pleased is as senseless as the assertion) and Olivi's doctrine does seem meaningless. Thus Jansen's road too is a cul-de-sac.

The verdict of meaninglessness remains unaltered if we judge that, though the Council fathers may have intended to condemn the doctrine Jansen describes, they did not in fact condemn Olivi's teaching, since both they and commentators like

Jansen misunderstood his teaching.[15] A mistake in attribution
would add nothing to the intelligibility of the doctrine denied
or of its negation. As a matter of historical fact, "even after
the Council, not just superficial observers but professional
theologians within the Franciscan order were convinced that
Olivi and his 'modern' theory had been 'condemned'."[16] But
others disagreed.[17] And disagreement has continued to our own
day, each firmly held interpretation being contradicted by another. As for the mass of Christians, they have of course never
understood what it is all about; "so that the revelation of all
these things has become . . . like the words of a scroll that is
sealed, which if one handed to a scholar with the request, 'Pray
read this,' he will say, 'I cannot, for it is sealed'; or if the scroll
be handed to one who is not a scholar, with the request, 'Pray
read this,' he will say, 'I am not a scholar' " (Is. 29, 11-12). No
meaning appears.

Suppose, though, as a final hypothesis, that my negative verdict on one of these three main alternatives is mistaken. Then
the situation would be somewhat similar to that I alluded to in
treating the second hypothesis. As no one variety of hylemorphism, if meaningful, would render the Council's teaching
meaningful, so here no one interpretation, if successful, would
automatically assure the meaningfulness of the Council's statements. For which of these three different approaches is the correct one? Each has something to say for it. And each has in
fact been followed. In purely pragmatic terms, and considering
solely the way the document has in fact been understood, we
find these three divergent interpretations. So shall we say that
the Council taught all three? Then its teaching is incoherent,
even in the supposition that one of the three interpretations is
not. And the same would hold for a disjunction of the three; for
a disjunction which contains even one meaningless member is
itself meaningless (e.g., "He was either angry, or drunk, or
raised to the square root of three."). Shall we say then that the
Council taught only one member of the disjunction—the coherent one? But on what grounds? I shall not inflict on the reader

a detailed examination of these various possibilities. It is enough to have demonstrated that all is not clear sailing even if one of the interpretations survives my criticism.

Nor shall I examine in detail the further suggestion that the force of the Council's declaration is legislative, not speculative, that is, that the Council did not teach a truth but forbade an objectionable manner of speaking (did not deny Olivi's doctrine but told him not to talk that way). For insofar as this hypothesis is defensible, it would seem to coincide with the one I have proposed, and in any case the result is the same: no doctrinal content. This is the important point here, not whether we attach the label "meaningful". For my interest is in the teaching office of the Church, not her legislation.

(b) The second sample to be considered is Pius XI's famous pronouncement on artificial birth control:

Assuredly no reason, even the most serious, can make congruent with nature and decent what is intrinsically against nature. Since the act of the spouses is by its own nature ordered to the generation of offspring, those who, exercising it, deliberately deprive it of its natural force and power, act against nature and effect what is base and intrinsically indecent. (AAS 22:559)

The Catholic Church, to whom God himself has committed the integrity and decency of morals, now standing in this ruin of morals, raises her voice aloud through our mouth, in sign of her divine mission, in order to keep the chastity of the nuptial bond free from this foul stain, and again promulgates: Any use whatever of marriage, in the exercise of which the act by human effort is deprived of its natural power of procreating life, violates the law of God and nature, and those who do such a thing are stained by a grave and mortal flaw. (AAS 22:560)[18]

(At nulla profecto ratio, ne gravissima quidem, efficere potest, ut, quod intrinsece est contra naturam, id cum natura congruens et honestum fiat. Cum autem actus coniugii suapte natura proli generandae sit destinatus, qui, in eo exercendo, naturali hac eum vi atque virtute de industria destituunt, contra naturam agunt et turpe quid atque intrinsece inhonestum operantur . . . Ecclesia catholica, cui ipse Deus morum integritatem honestatemque docendam et defendendam commisit, in media hac morum ruina posita, ut nuptialis foederis castimoniam a turpi hac labe immunem servet, in signum legationis suae divinae, altam per os Nostrum extollit vocem atque denuo promulgat: quemlibet matrimonii usum, in quo exercendo, actus, de industria hominum, naturali sua vitae procreandae vi destituatur, Dei et naturae legem infringere, et eos, qui tale quid commiserint, gravis noxae labe commaculari.)

A Catholic reading this solemn statement and agreeing with the encyclical's estimate of the historical situation would naturally feel bound to accept its verdict. Could so long and strong a tradition, capped by so weighty a declaration, be in error? During the years that followed the encyclical it came to seem to many that the choice lay between contraception and infallibility, so that to admit artificial contraception would be to deny infallibility. And once the option appeared in these terms, the issue could not remain in doubt; the verdict was necessarily that of *Humanae Vitae*. Those who have disagreed with that answer have not always understood the state of the question, and as a consequence have sometimes been unjust in their criticisms. Those critics who, on the contrary, have recognized the influence and force of the argument from tradition have sought to show that the absolute condemnation of artificial birth control is not a matter of faith. Neither side has envisaged a third possibility, that such a moral judgment may be unintelligible, and therefore neither true nor false.

A first difficulty concerns the act condemned. It is described as the act performed by onanists and non-onanists alike. Yet it is also called naturally procreative, which can hardly be said of the onanistic act. So is there some essence common to all the legitimate acts and to all the onanistic acts? But what essence, and why call it an act? I shall not insist on this difficulty here, for it seems clear enough what acts were intended, despite the unfortunate wording. And few readers have had any doubts on this score. True, they haven't generally noticed the incoherence. But suppose they had. Would they then have doubts? Should they? No, they would be in the same situation as those who heard the politician declaim about the flood-gates opened to a general conflagration, or the ecclesiastical orator regret the chasm erected between us. When practically all hearers discern without difficulty what the speaker means to say, the distinction between speaker's meaning and words' meaning disappears or becomes irrelevant. Communication takes place.

However, with regard to the moral terms employed no similar recourse is possible, to a familiar, evident meaning intended by the author. Neither the encyclical itself, nor the milieu from which it emerged, provides intelligible content for its declaration that onanistic intercourse is "base and intrinsically indecent", "a foul stain", a "grave and mortal flaw", which "violates the law of God and nature". For the encyclical provides no clearer lead than Vermeersch did as to what it means by "against nature". And the tradition to which they both belong offers various alternatives. And problems of sense arise for each.

As a first step in systematically surveying the situation, it should be noted again that Vermeersch was not just another moralist, more or less typical of a traditional approach. He was, writes Noonan, "the most influential moral theologian of the first part of the twentieth century", who "from 1918 to 1934 . . . dominated Roman moral theology", whose "role in stimulating the encyclical is evident", and whose "part in the drafting of the encyclical is not only known from its close conformity to his work, but may be inferred from the annotations he was able to publish on it within a month of its issuance".[19] He would seem in fact to be the man most likely to have actually penned the passage here being discussed. So failure to find intelligible content for his thesis on contraception, in his major work on sexual morality, has significance similar to the failure to find a meaning in Olivi for the Council of Vienne.

Still greater, however, was the influence of St. Thomas, which had been mounting steadily precisely during the years preceding the encyclical.[20] So it behooves us to consider the general drift of his thought on the question of contraception: "If coitus was to be regarded as an unalterable process because of its generative consequences, but not every act of coitus was generative, then a discrimination had to be made between the normal or per se and the accidental. This discrimination was made by Thomas. He postulated as normal an act of coitus which led to generation. This norm was not derived from any statistical compilation. It was the product of intuition, the same intellectual process by which Lactantius had concluded that the purpose of the sexual members was to generate. Because the sexual act might be generative, and because generation was an important function, the theologian intuited that generation was the normal function. A typical or essential act of coitus, which was generative, was therefore supposed. Other acts of coitus which did not achieve this purpose were regarded as generically generative but accidentally frustrated."[21]

To deal with this viewpoint, let us distinguish between a typical act and an essential act, as Noonan here suggests, and start with the former. The typical act is to be a norm of what is natural. It is because this act is naturally generative and the other is not that the other is "against nature". So let us suppose that the "typical" act is an unimpeded one, between fertile partners, during a fertile period. This choice fulfills most satisfactorily the requirement that the act be generative "of its very nature", and provides the most natural and intelligible meaning for that expression. The typical act is naturally generative because, and in the sense that, the spouses are fertile, at that very moment, and perform the act in a way that makes conception fairly likely. But now what will it mean to say that onanistic intercourse is against nature and is therefore immoral? Merely that it differs from the typical act (since conception is impeded in the one case, not in the other) and is therefore immoral (by definition). But this is hardly a satisfactory argument or explanation, or the one intended. So let us turn to the other alternative: an "essential act" which may serve as norm of what is natural.

If we distinguish between the one word "intercourse" and the various acts covered by it, then search for something common to them all, we find that the essence of intercourse belongs in the same class as the artichoke which has no leaves.[22] If we do find anything common to the acts, it is not common to them alone, nor does it suffice to constitute an act of intercourse, any more than the leafless nub suffices to constitute an artichoke. So let us look instead for some common formula (scholastic thinkers have, after all, tended to equate the enunciation of such a formula with the designation of an essence) and take as "essential act" any intercourse, whether onanistic or not, covered by the formula. The likeliest candidate is "coitus with insemination"; so let that be our essence. But in that case what is meant by calling the act naturally procreative? Many acts satisfy this definition yet are incapable of generating. And indeed many contraceptive acts fulfill the norm as perfectly as any others; insemination takes place. So why are they condemned? In what sense are they "against nature"? In this Thomistic direction, no solution appears.

Since no other author has a claim to our attention equal to that of St. Thomas or Vermeersch, and no other theoretical approach provides as likely a lead to the encyclical's sense, I shall pass to a third main alternative, corresponding to the first one considered for Vienne. " 'Evil', 'flaw', 'foul' and the like," it might be objected, "are not scholastic terms, requiring special knowledge on the part of the reader. They are ordinary words, understood by the ordinary person, in their ordinary sense. Complicated, perhaps confused reasoning may have preceded their use in the encyclical, but the resulting statements are perfectly intelligible in themselves. If a person tells me an action is wrong, I know what he means without knowing his reasons. And the same is true for the encyclical. So your criticisms seem mere quibbling."

This is a natural objection. So let us get clear about its sense. Does it mean that there is an "ordinary meaning" of moral terms, distinct from the meanings encountered in moral theology, and that despite the encyclical's references to nature and nature's law, we should ignore the natural-law tradition and consult the man in the street for the encyclical's true meaning? Hardly. Does it mean then that if we look beneath the evident diversity in terminology, criteria, methods, and conclusions, we shall find that moralists all share common moral concepts with the man in the street? The hypothesis lacks sense. But even if it were intelligible, is it something we are to believe *a priori*, or in virtue of a vague intuition, or has it actually been discovered *a posteriori* through a thorough, analytic survey of moral discourse and moral writings? About the degree of underlying uniformity there may be debate,[23] but this at least is clear, that nobody has actually established, empirically, that massive uniformity does exist. Whence then the vague impression that it does, and that we can fall back on it in interpreting a document like *Casti Connubii*?[24]

I can think of no more instructive comparison here than James's treatment of truth, analyzed in Chapter Four. When James insisted that truth is a process and not the static relation alleged by his adversaries, he thus made it perfectly clear that he and they were not talking about the same thing when they spoke of "truth". For process and static relation are opposed as black and white, and what one color is both black and white? Yet James drew no such conclusion. Nor has anyone I have discussed the matter with. James's readers, too, suppose that he presented a counter-theory, clashing with the traditional correspondence theory. For after all, both he and his opponents were talking about *truth*. So apparently there must be some one thing which his adversaries maintained was a static relation and he held was a process. But what could it possibly be? "Well, *truth*." When a person has received that sort of answer just often enough, he begins to sympathize with Wittgenstein's desperate plea: "Don't think, but look!" Free yourself from mere words. If we manage to banish *a priori* assumptions and simply open our eyes and minds to reality, we shall no longer imagine that philosophers all refer to the same thing and just differ in their descriptions when one calls truth a process, another calls it correspondence between mind and reality, and still others argue that it is subjectivity, coherence, use-usage correspondence, and so on. When just two doctrines are in question, it is easy for people to suppose some common reference; but the error becomes unmistakable when the list grows to half a dozen or more incompatible "theories".

The same approach leads to similar conclusions in ethics, where equal diversity reigns, thickly veiled by words. When some Pharisee, let us imagine, invoked Yahweh's rest on the seventh day and Jesus replied, "But what of this woman's health?",[25] they were not arguing about some third, unnamed thing, the rightness or wrongness of curing her on the Sabbath. Their moral terms did not have a common reference, which one side affirmed and the other denied. For what would the common reference be? Once again, let us not say, "Well, rightness or wrongness." That is no answer. Rather, let us *look*, and consider various alternatives. Jesus weighed the woman's health against the values represented by the Sabbath, or by Sabbath observance as then interpreted, and found that the scales tipped in her favor. So let us try defining the rightness of an act as the prevalence of value over disvalue in a given situation. Is this, then, what the Pharisees too were talking about? Were they going on the assumption that if Yahweh rested on the Sabbath, then surely it is best for human beings to rest on the Sabbath, and get themselves healed some other time, no matter what their condition? Was the argument from Genesis really connected in their thinking, if not in their words, with the prevalence of value over disvalue, and did they just consider the quasi-historical clue a surer guide to the welfare of individuals than any considerations of their immediate circumstances? Of course not. But if the value criterion was not the common reference, guaranteeing sameness of meaning to Jesus' terms and theirs, what was? What third thing called rightness or wrongness did he think was connected with values and they with the account of Genesis? Can the reader think of anything? Does he have any reason to suppose there *had* to be something? No, these blinkers must come off. Jesus and his adversaries may have used the same terminology, but there is no good reason to suppose that they were talking about the same thing and just differing in their judgments about it.[26] If there is any one thing they were talking about it was the action, and they disagreed on whether to do it, not about whether it possessed a certain property indicated by their common moral terms.

Now Jesus' mode of moral reasoning is, fortunately, widespread. Not only would the man in the street tend to agree with him, but natural-law thinkers, too, though they may slight the particular case, frequently try to balance pluses and minuses in reaching a general verdict. So should we perhaps interpret *Casti Connubii* in the light of this widespread tendency, and say that the encyclical ignored such evidence but was really talking about the same thing? It does not explicitly state that what is against nature is consistently harmful to man, but does it perhaps take the connection for granted? Well, does the antecedent literature in which we find a similar silence also take the connection for granted? What of all the authors who made no attempt to work out a correlation between naturalness and the consistent prevalence of varied values, or between unnaturalness and the consistent, universal prevalence of disvalue? Are we to suppose that this constant correlation, though in fact inconceivable, appeared self-evident to them, so unworthy of even passing mention? Anyone familiar with this tradition knows how unrealistic such suppositions are. These authors, when they discussed contraception, were not working within a broad perspective of balancing values and disvalues. Nor, therefore, did their terms have such meanings.

If the reader feels that my general thesis of diversity in moral meaning requires fuller proof than these few samples, he has missed their significance. The thesis that would have to be proved is that of uniformity, for the appearances are all against it. So are the *a priori* probabilities. For the common criteria, notice, though perhaps not reflectively recognized as constituting a common meaning, would necessarily be familiar to all; hidden features, or secrets known to only a few, form no part of any concept. Yet this common something, present in all uses of moral terms and guiding our employment of them, would be so well concealed from philosophers' reflective gaze that no one has ever detected it. Even were such a hypothesis intelligible, it would not be plausible. So we may without qualms focus on the encyclical itself, to surmise what it, at least, was talking about. The key phrase, I have suggested, is "against nature". But that expression is not elucidated, either by the encyclical or by the tradition from which it derives. Thus no light—no meaning—appears.

Reflecting back over the course of this discussion concerning *Casti Connubii* and of the previous one concerning Vienne, the reader may feel inclined to object: "Doesn't it come to this: you reject these documents because *you* cannot understand hylemorphism and *you* cannot make sense out of the natural-law arguments against artificial contraception. But other people have. So how have you proved that the documents are meaningless?" My answer is, first, that to believe one understands is not to understand; and, second, that a demand for proof would suggest that the situation had been misconceived.

Suppose someone were to say, "I have calculated π to eighty places and have not encountered three consecutive sevens; I conclude, therefore, that such a sequence does not occur in the development of π." That would be a hasty verdict, to say the least; the sought-for sequence might occur in the next eighty places. And no number of calculations, however great, would make its discovery less likely. But suppose that someone were to say: "I've looked in the clothespress and under the bed and conclude that nobody is in the room." You would not treat this argument with similar contempt, or require a rigorous proof, especially if the clothespress and the bed were the room's main furnishings. Now what I have done in both these cases, Vienne and *Casti Connubii*, is to look in the likeliest places. And if someone is still inclined to object, "But what about the curtains?", then my reply is: "What curtains?" The burden of proof, it seems to me, now rests with the objector. He should either indicate an important alternative I have overlooked and show that it reveals the document's sense, or demonstrate that some explanation I have rejected deserves closer scrutiny. However, as I suggested at the start, even if someone did succeed better than I have in one of these two places—Vienne and *Casti Connubii*—what about the rest of the magisterial mansion? Is it likely that every room where a first examination reveals no occupant nevertheless contains one, cunningly concealed? What reason have we to make such a supposition?

"If it is thus," I can imagine someone replying, "what good is the Church's teaching? What difference does it make, for instance, whether *Casti Connubii* was wrong or merely meaningless? Isn't the effect the same? If theologians subsequently ignored this third alternative, wasn't their attitude the only realistic one? How could they suppose that the flock of Christ, turning to its pastor for food, had been given a mere placebo—or meaningless poison?" The apparent strength of this objection is one reason for my choosing to consider the contraception example. Here, if anywhere, is a case which might seem to indicate how perilous is the thesis that magisterial statements may be meaningless.

The Improbability of Divine Protection

The decisive answer to such misgivings and such objections is that the need for protection against error in a given case cannot be converted into a guarantee of protection in every case. And as for individual cases which may seem crucial, the need for protection becomes much more dubious when we turn from the traditional true-false dichotomy to the distinction between meaningful and meaningless and to the perspective of mixed advantages and disadvantages which characterizes it. These are the points which I shall develop in the present section, starting with the last.

The consequences of meaningless words vary from beneficial to harmless to harmful, along a varied continuum. In the majority of cases it would be absurd to equate a lapse in meaning with the triumph of hell's gates against Christ's Church. The overall effect of all such statements combined may be negative, but even that is not evident *a priori*, and it would not demonstrate the need of universal protection. On the whole, we might compare meaningless magisterial statements with colds; they are unfortunately common, but hardly threaten life, save perhaps in exceptional circumstances.

This is what one might suspect *a priori*. For a statement which is meaningless does not consistently misinform, if it informs or influences at all. The cognitive effects are likely to be as mixed and muddled as the meaning, with good effects balancing the bad. However, I had better demonstrate in some detail, *a posteriori*, that such is the case; for I can easily imagine someone having a contrary *a priori* impression. Since meaning is more basic than truth, lack of meaning might seem a more total, drastic failing than lack of truth. After all, quite intelligent people err about difficult matters, and slip into falsehood, but at least they don't talk nonsense! This reaction is understandable but mistaken; for the fact is that if one cannot reach the level of truth, it is usually better not to reach even the level of meaning. If a proposition isn't true, it is better that it had never been born. Still-born nonsense is preferable.

The samples from this and previous chapters provide varied illustration of this truth. For instance, starting with the simpler paradigms:

1. The interviewer in Chapter Two, #12, though he loses five

minutes and perhaps his patience, has a good story to tell and acquires new insight into human nature.

2. The mischievous mathematician in #9 may have achieved precisely what he intended, despite the fact that his statement was literal nonsense. If he does in fact have numerous friends in the department, and his interlocutor, hearing that their number equals the cube root of 383, concludes that they are numerous, the result is a true belief, though the statement is neither true nor false. But let us pass to more relevant cases.

3. Although the claim is sometimes made for the doctrine of formal causality (discussed in Chapter Four, #5) that it alone saves man's unity, few people, I imagine, have required reassurance on that score. But I suspect that many people have felt the need for some identifiable item of their human make-up to serve as subject of survival if the doctrine of life after death was to be meaningful and believable for them. Consider, for example, how alarmed were Socrates' companions in the *Phaedo* at the prospect that the soul was really the body's harmony, which would perish with the body. The admission would have amounted to no more than the transfer of a label, with no consequences for survival. But people are so little aware of the difference between conceptual and substantive issues that the creation of a label like "substantial form" can assume great importance in their eyes. Thus I feel sure that a good many people, when they start to doubt the hylemorphic doctrine, suppose immortality to be implicated in their doubts. To bolster their hylemorphism is to bolster their faith, much as in the case of Socrates' disciples. This benefit may perhaps balance the considerable confusion generated by the doctrine.

4. It is clear that James used his theory of truth (Chapter Four, #6) to turn people's attention to consequences; and that is a healthy turn. However, when brought about in this way, concern for consequences is inevitably one-sided. The definition not only converts people to the values it includes, but away from the values it omits. Thus thinking like James's has played a part in the one-sidedly pragmatic interpretation of doctrine

which is so widespread today. These effects may be fairly even-
ly matched: the benefit of greater realism versus neglect of
truth; immediate pastoral relevance versus ultimate pastoral
ruin when and if the cognitive foundation of practice disappears. Other effects, of a more theoretical sort, would be obfus-
cation of the concept "true", on the one hand, with all the ramifications such clouding can have, and on the other hand the
conversion of some people from still more nebulous thinking.
In comparison with some systems, James's pragmatism is
sound good sense; in comparison with others, it is a hopeless
muddle. So who is to say whether James's chapter on truth did
more harm or good?

5. The verdict for a magisterial statement may be equally
problematic. Consider, for instance, the definition of Vienne,
concerning the human soul. On the mass of the faithful, who
can make nothing of such terminology, it has no immediate effect. Those who have thought they understood it have perhaps
been affected in the same way as those who thought they understood James. If it weaned some from Olivi to Thomas, fine.
If it confirmed others in an incoherent doctrine of formal causality, not so fine. The results perhaps balance out. And in any
case, they are hardly catastrophic.

Once it is seen that the presence or absence of meaning in
magisterial statements is not a matter of life and death but
merely of better and worse, there remains only the argument
that it would be better for the Church's teaching to always
make sense, so God must have granted this favor. And concerning such a defense as that, I agree with C. S. Lewis:
"There is one argument which we should beware of using
for either position: God must have done what is best, this is
best, therefore God has done this. For we are mortals and do
not know what is best for us, and it is dangerous to prescribe
what God must have done—especially when we cannot, for the
life of us, see that He has after all done it."[27]

Familiarity with what, in the history of thought, have passed
as good, even convincing rebuttals warns me, however, to deal

at least briefly with one or two specious arguments against my thesis. I can, for instance, imagine someone harboring misgivings like these: "In this supposition *Casti Connubii* would be a horrible mistake, of a sort which hardly seems compatible with the Church's indefectibility. So the supposition must be wrong." Here two confusions need to be straightened out. First, the objection fails to distinguish between the denial of blanket protection and the blanket denial of protection; I have not excluded the possibility that in some cases, at least, divine help may be needed if disastrous consequences are to be avoided. Second, the objector, not I, makes the crucial supposition that the encyclical was catastrophic, and if he is right about that, his unwanted conclusion follows in any case, regardless of my thesis or my analysis of the encyclical's meaning.

It is still more probable that misgivings will arise from reasoning like the following: if magisterial statements may be meaningless, and if the lack of meaning is typically so well veiled, then we could never know whether a given doctrine makes sense; and the net result would be perplexity about each and every item of revelation, each and every utterance of the magisterium. Meaning must be universally assured, therefore, if the Church is to exercise her teaching function effectively. Allow one meaningless statement and all become suspect.

Notice, though, that the thing to be established is divine intervention, not our belief in divine intervention, and a proof of divine intervention based on our need to believe it would not only be a defective argument but psychologically ineffectual. It would be the mental equivalent of pulling oneself up by one's bootstraps. Besides, a meaning which no one can find is no better than a non-existent meaning. And if people are sure it exists, it is rather worse; for then they waste their time in a fruitless search, whereas they would give up after a reasonable effort if they envisaged the possibility that the statement was meaningless.

So let us accept our mortality and adopt the attitude towards meaning we take towards truth: not guilty until proved guilty;

not suspect until grounds for suspicion are solidly established. As the falsehood of earlier widespread views about Jewish observances, the date of the parousia, the arrangement of the planets, the origin of man, biblical forms and authorship, and so on, showed that the views were not revealed truths, as many had believed, nor essential for salvation, so now equally convincing evidence that a given doctrine is incoherent may have a similar effect. Progress in the study of language may have repercussions similar to those of astronomy, geology, biology, history, archeology, and the study of ancient literature. Thus a future generation, made more aware of language and its complexities, may come to view our present attitude towards magisterial statements as a species of fundamentalism, akin to the attitude towards Scripture which currently goes by that name. Only gradually and with great difficulty has the lesson concerning Scripture been conveyed to faithful and theologians alike: the word of God is also the word of man.

Conclusion

Underlying aims and fears are often more decisive for or against the acceptance of a thesis like the one just proposed than are explicit arguments. My own motives will appear more clearly in the next chapter. Here, in conclusion, I would like to consider briefly two chief reactions which are likely to create resistance to my proposal.

One is the reasonable expectation that it will lead to abuses and misunderstandings. True, the preceding arguments warrant no ready inference to the possibility of meaningless *ex cathedra* statements, still less to their existence. Nor do they produce any reason to question the central truths of faith. However, without any sure norm to go by, may not some readers start to wonder? And won't others be only too glad to use this ready-made instrument to eliminate whatever doctrine displeases them?

Such expectations, I say, are reasonable. For consider the recent course of biblical scholarship. Told that some books of the Bible are not historical, people did in fact start wondering about the gospels. Told that the gospels themselves are not history in the modern sense of the term, they wondered about the most central events of salvation history. Informed, now, that the resurrection itself was not a historical event in the sense that, say, the crucifixion was, they do indeed wonder whether it "ever happened". And the answers of some theologians and exegetes, at this stage in the development, probably do undermine the very foundations of Christian faith. Now it is conceivable that the type of inquiry I have illustrated should eventually lead to some such consequences. But is that any reason to halt the process at the start? Would it really have been better to impose biblical fundamentalism forever?

As for the absence of any sure norm—any precise definition of sense or precise criterion of when a statement lacks sense— consider a similar parallel. "Scripture," declares the fundamentalist, "is the unexceptionable, unquestionable Word of God." "But it is also the word of man," replies the non-fundamentalist; "it expresses some merely human views along with the divine. Think, for instance, of St. Paul's ideas about women and their dress, or the instructions to the church of Antioch, or the early attitude towards slavery, or belief in the Lord's quick return." The fundamentalist would find this answer disturbing. Where will such a suggestion end? Reflecting on the varied examples cited, he perhaps decides that a definition is what he needs. So he replies: "What do you mean by 'human opinions'? And how do you define the difference between 'word of God' and 'word of man'? In its present vague state, your proposal looks dangerous." To this the other might reply: "Any definition general enough to cover all the varied cases I've mentioned, plus others, would be far less illuminating than the examples themselves, and it would provide no method for determining what was word of man, what word of God. All the real problems would remain." This is roughly how

I regard my own suggestion concerning magisterial statements and their meaningfulness. The precision of general formulae is illusory, the precision of examples is not. And I have provided examples.

General acceptance of my thesis may also depend, I suspect, on how important people consider it that the Church, the hierarchy, or the pope should never lose face. To someone who has tended to think of Jesus in lofty and abstract terms, the hypothesis that he sometimes caught a cold may sound almost blasphemous. And for someone who has thought of the Church as Christ's bride and of the pope as Christ's vicar on earth, the thesis that magisterial statements sometimes lack meaning may sound similarly shocking. But muddles, like colds, are the common lot of the race in which God has become incarnate. And I would hope that one and all—Church, hierarchy, and Christ's vicar—would place themselves no higher than their master, but would reply with him as he did to those who had expected something more magnificent: "Blessed are those who are not scandalized in me."

CHAPTER SIX

Wider Horizons

would be surprised if some readers
did not react to the previous chapter
much as people did to the work of
Loisy: there are many Catholics, said William Barry, "not in
any sense personally hostile, who feel that when he has completed the task of dissection, nothing definite, nothing sufficiently solid, will be left on which to build dogmatic religion."[1] And if such is the likely reaction of theologians and
others who might be expected to read a book like this, is it not
probable that the mass of the faithful will be still more adverse-
ly affected if they ever hear about my thesis? Their reaction
would be mistaken, and would result from misconceptions, it is
true, but wouldn't the scandal be more harmful than the misconceptions? And is this really the opportune moment to cast
obloquy on the magisterium? Isn't the bark of Peter rocking
enough without further stirring the waters?

So should we temporarily bury our heads in the boat, till the
storm blows over? If so, at least we should not mistake the pos-
ture for Christian faith or call it loyalty to Christ. The Lord
Jesus himself did much sifting and sorting, both of what was
commonly regarded as God's plan for his people and of what
was proposed as the unadulterated word of God, with the result

that he was abandoned by the nationalistic masses and punished for his impiety by the guardians of the law. Their indignation was heightened by a strongly symbolic act: the cleansing of the Temple.

Intervention was required, they said, lest such agitation upset the delicate political balance on which the nation's welfare depended. They might also have urged, and probably did, that with Hellenism threatening to engulf God's chosen people and their one true faith, an unbroken front of practice and belief was called for and not disruptive poking and probing. But Jesus was undeterred by such considerations. He evidently judged that the truth was what they needed most of all.

These observations do not yet amount to a defense of my own probings or prove they are analogous. But they may serve as a reminder that God's designs are not always what we suppose them to be, and that human nature has not been altered all that radically by Christ's coming, either in its temptations or in its genuine needs. In this concluding chapter, I shall note some major contemporary needs and relate them to the preceding study, starting with the need for truth.

"Anything That Is Made Visible Is Light"

Every researcher, every inquirer in whatever field, can understand, by analogy, the reply of Mallory, when asked why he wished to scale Mount Everest: "Because it is there." There are Himalayas which the human mind must scale, simply because they are there. And if the natural-law line of thought has any validity, it should warn us against too readily adopting the attitude: "You don't belong on those mountains; someone is likely to get killed." The history of mankind is a story of ever new horizons, opened by people who ran the risk of being killed, literally or figuratively, and often were.

The new land, the new universe, the new invention or way of life or view of things has often seemed alarming at the start.

Automobiles were terrifying, man was not meant to fly, the infinite reaches of time and space begot Pascalian shivers, the theories of Darwin and Einstein made the solid earth of common sense tremble beneath people's feet. But then they became accustomed to the new way, the new view, the new invention. It began to shed light instead of darkness, to give comfort rather than pain. Now many wonder how they could ever have done without television or the automobile, or have lived in the cramped and static universe of the ancients, or have properly appreciated Scripture without knowledge of its history and forms.

Consider, too, the things we have always taken for granted, for instance stupidity, or sin. Innocent lack of meaning will hardly destroy the Church if moral evil has not. And serious moral lapses there have been, from the days of Judas on. But we accept this fact unquestioningly, it is so evident and familiar. Lack of meaning, however, though far less of a threat to the well-being of the Church or mankind, troubles us. For that fact, as ancient and perhaps as pervasive as the other, we have not noticed nor grown accustomed to. It seems terrible, even heretical, to suggest that incoherence or lack of meaning might slip into Church documents.

My point in making this comparison is not to repeat the argument of the previous chapter, but to suggest once more, as in the preceding parallels, that initial dismay is likely to be short-lived and that the sooner the step is taken the better.[2] For imagine that the fact of moral evil in the Church were unknown or ignored. Would that be for our good? Would it be wise to keep the fact hidden, lest the faithful be scandalized? They would then no longer consider themselves sinners, or even potential sinners. In their dealings with fellow-Christians, whether superiors, subordinates, or equals, children, parents, teachers, students, pastors, bishops or popes, they would give no thought to the scandalous suggestion that they or the others might *sin*! Heaven (literally) forbid!

The suggestion is, of course, absurd; but that is its value. I am employing the Wittgensteinian technique of passing from obvious nonsense to hidden nonsense, and showing it to be such. If difficulties of meaning are as common as sin, should this fact of life be kept from people whereas sin is freely admitted? For what reason? That it would be too awful an admission? But our sinfulness is an infinitely worse accusation. Or because the fact is not a fact, but a mere hypothesis, and we need not hurry to beat our breasts when our lapses in meaning are perhaps far fewer than our lapses in virtue? But then the defect to be acknowledged is less fearful, and the admission still less of a disgrace.

To the discovery of sin and to the other discoveries I have cited (evolution, solar system, literary forms, etc.) the words of Scripture apply: "When anything is exposed by the light, it is made visible, and anything that is made visible is light" (Eph. 5, 13). Sin itself is illuminating if we have the honesty and courage to recognize it in ourselves and in the Church. The Curé of Ars, it is said, asked to see the extent of his sinfulness fully revealed, without the customary veil of complacency and self-deception. The revelation, we are told, was harrowing. But his request was not mistaken. Why, then, should we take any other attitude towards our possible failures with respect to meaning? Shouldn't our prayer be similar: "Lord, let us see clearly how much we fail to see clearly, how confused our thoughts and sayings are, how unfounded our complacent assumptions of lucidity and understanding. As our sinfulness camouflages our sins, so our confusion veils our nonsense. Only you can wipe the mist entirely from our eyes."

The question which I have had to consider as I wrote was this: Are the words I have quoted from Ephesians quite generally true? Do they apply here too? Does everything which is brought to light shed light? The problem I have been treating is a dark place of theology, there is no doubt of that. But should we leave dark places dark, for fear of what we may find in them? Then we disagree with the final part of the quotation; things made visible are *not* light. God has done or permitted things which it is better for us not to know about! Compared to a thesis such as that, surely mine is innocuous. And notice that the basic issue here is not whether my thesis is right or wrong; if I was to investigate the matter at all, I had to attempt an answer and therefore risk being wrong, whichever conclusion I reached. "The first step in settling a question of doctrine," wrote Newman, "is to raise and debate it."[3]

The Realm of Meaning

Till now I have mentioned only the importance of the question in itself, and though that is considerable, I suspect that the wider implications of this study are still more important. For one thing, the conclusions of Chapter Five concerning magisterial pronouncements are applicable to the faith of the Church as a whole. Yet the parallel is not perfect. It will be necessary to follow Wittgenstein's example once again and, while using the study of magisterial statements as a model, note dissimilarities as well as similarities.

I made two main points about magisterial statements: first, that some are likely to be meaningless, unless all are divinely protected, and second, that I see no good reason to suppose such universal protection. Both of these conclusions, and the arguments for them, hold as well for the faith of the Church, whether stated in official texts or not. If anything, the mass of Christians are on the whole less reflective about language and meaning than those who draw up Church documents; and possible incoherence among those taught is no more disastrous than incoherence in official documents which do some of the teaching.

Such is the general picture, but let us look more closely into the details of the comparison. I have suggested more than once that awareness of language becomes especially necessary in speculative discussion, and that incoherence is more likely in an explanation of the Trinity or a theory of grace than in an inquiry about the weather. But the average Catholic or Christian does not engage in speculation. So isn't he safer? Isn't he less likely to become confused in his thoughts? His staples are Scripture, liturgy, the lives of saints.

True, but we are discussing his beliefs, and these he receives, for instance, from the catechism, or from a sermon in church, or from a religion or theology course in school. And in these places theology and the magisterium have a strong influence. They filter down. Perhaps only a minority of those to whom *Casti Connubii* was addressed ever studied natural-law arguments such as lay behind it, but one way or another all got the message: contraception was wrong! But did this message make better sense when it reached them than it had at the start? When the doctrine entered simpler minds, did it get straightened out?

An extremely interesting question, that, with far-reaching implications. One thing seems clear: the message that reached them did not turn them all into scholastic, natural-law philosophers on the spot. Even supposing that a coherent natural-law interpretation of the encyclical's terms was worked out, it is evident that no such sense was communicated to the majority of the faithful. Nor, for that matter, did they ever hold such a common faith in the past. Only if, in this case as in some others, scholastic philosophy simply put common thoughts in order, could such a claim be made. And I have already indicated that this was far from the case. Moral judgments are typically based on benefits to man. In this the mainstream of Christian moral thinking concurs: let them have life! And the categorical rejection of contraception, both in *Casti Connubii* and in the tradition behind it, was based on a very different approach.

Such reflections open up a new dimension in the contraception debate, and by implication in many another discussion as well. To a great extent it has been enough for theologians if everyone said the same words. Vincent of Lerins' rule was then satisfied: everyone agreed, so it was a matter of faith. But let us ask, in simplified terms: If for a fifth of the faithful "X is wrong" means "Don't do it," and for another fifth "It's been forbidden," and for another "It's bad for you," and for another "It's against nature," and for a final fifth nothing at all, what are they all agreeing on? Do they believe the same thing? Suppose it so happened that you couldn't say all these things with one word ("wrong"): would this accident of language prevent a common faith? Well, does the actual linguistic situation *establish* a common faith? Does it make no difference how widely diverse the doctrines are, provided you can find an expression which covers them all? Well, in what language? Latin? And why not simply make up an expression for the purpose? I know the saying about the questions a fool can ask, but this too is a Wittgensteinian procedure. I want the reader to realize that there is a problem here, a very basic one, and one which has not received due attention. For it is linguistic, analytic, semantic. And that is the neglected dimension.

Let us alter the model now: philosophers and theologians develop a complex theory of natural law, conclude to a condemnation of contraception, promulgate it through the magisterium to the mass of the faithful, who understand it uniformly, but in an entirely different sense. Knowing nothing about natural-law theory, they suppose, for instance, that contraception conflicts with man's supernatural end. Thus they say what their teachers say, and act as intended, but for them the word "wrong" has a different meaning, at least in this application, than it does for those who formulated the doctrine. May we then speak of the "common faith of the Church" and use this consensus as further proof that the doctrine taught was indeed a revealed truth?

I do not propose this as an accurate picture of events, nor even as a decent caricature. My aim, once again, is to indicate a type of problem deserving attention. For Wittgenstein's observation applies in theology too: "If I had to say what is the main mistake made by philosophers of the present generation, including Moore, I would say that it is that when language is looked at, what is looked at is a form of words and not the use made of the form of words."[4] There is failure, for instance, to recognize the complexity and diversity of moral discourse.

More precisely, a common error is to suppose that whereas the reasons for moral judgments may vary greatly, when, in the conclusion to an argument, we call an action good or bad, moral or immoral, the sense of these terms remains quite unaffected by the reasons adduced. It is as though we were calling them red or blue, one person because he preferred blue, another because he had heard they were blue, a third because he had seen a picture, a fourth because he had inspected them, a fifth because he knew the pigments used, and so on. Good is good and bad is bad, just as red is red and blue is blue, whatever one's reasons for making the judgment. But this will not do. How much truth such claims contain, I have suggested in Chapter Three; how much error, I have tried to show both there and in Chapter Five. Words get their meanings from their uses, and the uses of moral terms are varied, vague, and extraordinarily complex. They lie at the opposite pole from "red" and "blue".

Now what does all this have to do with the thesis of this book, that magisterial statements may be meaningless? This: whoever accepts or even takes seriously the possibility that magisterial statements, and not just pious ejaculations or the writings of individual theologians, may have not only a blurred or puzzling meaning but no meaning at all, can hardly fail to realize that meaning is indeed problematic. I have gone all the way. I have stated the strongest thesis of all, with the expectation that even those readers who remain skeptical about this claim may at least start puzzling over meaning as they never have before. And to help open up this unfamiliar territory, I have provided more background material than was strictly necessary for the magisterial samples analyzed.

In Defense of Mystery

The manner in which I have just discussed contraception— the rapid-fire questions without answers, the shifting perspectives, ever new complications and the hint of others whenever we trouble to glance beneath the surface of words—all this, I say, may have strengthened the impression that the words I quoted from William Barry were indeed apt: "Nothing definite, nothing sufficiently solid, will be left on which to build dogmatic religion." Now, in a certain sense I would consider this result a blessing, but in another sense it would contradict the whole thrust of this book. While some bypass the cognitive aspect of religious language, I have made it my sole concern. Whereas they tend to translate dogmatic statements into life-formulae, I have given an objective, factual interpretation. While they perhaps shudder at the very word "magisterium", I have taken magisterial statements as my focal topic. And not to destroy, but to fulfill. To bring new perfection to our understanding of the faith. And this means, perhaps first and foremost, accepting mystery.[5]

Thus, in a sense, I accept the verdict. The analytic approach I have proposed and exemplified is indeed opposed to a certain sort of definiteness, a certain sort of solidity, a certain sort of dogmatic religion. I view with misgivings the idea that we can build up dogma in the sense of improving on original revelation. Sometimes we can, sometimes we can't. But I am distrustful of the notion that if we just use our wits we can get a sharper view of *transcendent* reality. To illustrate more clearly what sort of "improvements" I fear, and the kind of definiteness and solidity I oppose, here is another paradigm—a true case, this time, and typical of thousands of others.

An acquaintance of mine once told his parish priest that he couldn't believe in the real presence of Christ in the Eucharist or in transubstantiation. His pastor replied that in that case he should leave the Church. And he did. A simple tale, all too familiar. But what lessons it has to teach! It contains the secret of so many crises of faith, and a perfect portrait of the tradition which nurtures them. If this is definiteness, if this is solidity, we have had far too much of both.

I am speaking, mind you, of both men. They both knew just what they were talking about, and one couldn't swallow it, whereas the other had a "stronger faith". There is the tragic error. "*What* can't you believe?", one would like to ask the doubter. And to the pastor one would like to say: "Why didn't *you* ask him that?" But the answer is plain enough: the priest shared the same presuppositions.

The tendencies revealed are so common, so powerful. I was teaching a religion class once and had discussed the Real Presence. "But you don't mean to say," a bright boy exclaimed, "that there are two kinds of presence!" There you have it in a nutshell. That is why the man left the Church and why his pastor let him go. They had a single, simple model, which didn't seem to fit—and didn't!—but one felt sure it was wrong and left, whereas the other held on with a tenacious but misguided faith, ruinous to the other if not to himself. The answer to the boy, and to both the men, is: "There are a hundred and one familiar varieties of presence, and the Real Presence is doubtless not one of them." Think of the ways we use the word "in": "in debt", "in time", "in love", "in town", "in deep water", "in the care of", "in sorrow and shame", "in a hurry", "in trouble", "in the race", "in competition with", and countless others. (Consider the variety of senses, not just the variety of objects the preposition takes.)

With this general introduction, let us reflect more attentively on the doubter in the tale, since he is so typical. Crises and problems of faith, as opposed for instance to deterioration in one's awareness of the supernatural, arise through apparent conflicts between doctrine and reality or within doctrine itself. And such apparent conflict is possible only if we have a fairly definite notion of just what the doctrine means. For mysteries are not hard enough to clash, not precise enough to conflict. The gears fail to mesh when we interpret a doctrine more definitely, in terms of some simple, familiar paradigm. It is the same thing as happens so often in philosophy, where Socrates, for example, feeling sure each word has a definition and designates an essence, sought in vain for the leafless artichoke. On the one hand it seems that there must be such a thing, but on the other hand there just isn't. So, too, Christians are troubled time and again by just such simple, misleading models of how things are or must be. When they realize or come to suspect that they aren't, they either "lose their faith" or grit their teeth and hang on. It is this sad state of affairs that I would remedy. And the only remedy is to realize the truth of Wittgenstein's words, especially with regard to the doctrines of faith: "Words are like the film on deep water." Deep, deep water, and no one sees the bottom. The man who thinks he does is looking at his own reflection.

Let us turn now to the priest who hung on, despite his misconceptions, revealed in his handling of the case. "Surely *he* knew better," you may say, "and that is why he had no such difficulties. After all, even a good catechism points out the difference between ordinary, physical presence and Christ's eucharistic presence. And the priest had studied theology." Yes, and what theology! The man's pastor was representative of his training, and his training was representative of a long tradition. The difference between this priest and his parishioner was the difference between a scientific and a non-scientific version of the same basic error.

To illustrate the error I have in mind, in a way which indicates clearly, I think, what the error is and that it is an error and one which has characterized much theology through many centuries, I shall adopt the following expedient. Let us imagine that a sighted man, like one in the paradigm previously examined,[6] has described a color to the congenitally blind: "Scarlet, he tells them, "is, as it were, a trumpet note." His hearers, naturally, are somewhat mystified by this saying, and after a time seek to understand the mystery they are asked to believe. A first firm step is apparently taken when they reach agreement on this formulation: "There is a *real resemblance* between trumpet notes and scarlet." The appearance of clarity and precision increases when someone notes and all concur that a trumpet note has not only timbre but volume and pitch, and that therefore it is necessary to say: "There is a real resemblance between scarlet and a *whole* trumpet note—timbre, volume, and pitch." This advance then permits further scientific developments in the doctrine. It is suggested, for instance, that if scarlet is, in a sense, a trumpet note, then in a certain sense it is not a color, for a trumpet note is a sound, not a color, and scarlet resembles it. This discovery is then enunciated as the doctrine of *trans-categorization*, which naturally causes doubts and difficulties among the faithful, but is affirmed as a matter of revealed truth. And in a sense it is. For the Seer called scarlet a trumpet note.

I shall not continue the rich and varied history of this doctrine—the wealth of analysis to which it was subjected, the great variety of explanations offered, the theories and counter-theories, the subtle distinctions and precise terminology. To them it all seemed deadly serious and scientific. But to the one who saw, it provided some wistful amusement. But also concern. For their blindness to color was not tragic, but blindness to their blindness could be dangerous. And that of course was their error. They thought there was some substitute for eyes. Or rather, they thought very little about what they were doing. They just wanted to see. But the only way they could see was through the eyes of one who did. They would never learn more about the look of scarlet than he communicated to them. No rewording of theirs, or technical elaboration, could ever improve on his simple words.

Anyone familiar with Eucharistic doctrine and its development will know what parallels I have in mind. Christ said (something like) "This is my body, this is the chalice of my blood." These words are as deeply mysterious to us as would be the description of scarlet to a man born blind. But we would see, would understand. In particular, the tradition of Western thought in which Catholic theology developed has been adverse to nebulous thoughts. The doctrine had to be given precision, solidity, sureness. Yet no reformulation could possibly improve on the first. There could be no question of clarifying the original statement, or sharpening it. For can the blind improve on the well-chosen words of one who sees? A careful reformulation in the language of a later day may indeed be helpful to convey the original message or counter some heresy. But to the extent that new formulae give the impression of somehow improving on the original, they are dangerous. And we would be laboring under a delusion if we supposed that theological reflection might provide a more exact understanding of this mystery than was conveyed to the apostles by the Master's simple words. Theologians must reflect carefully on their own language-game, and so learn how and in what sense they can be truly scientific.

The simple model I have been using is helpful in this respect. For it has a balanced, double effect. On the one hand it counteracts the false definiteness, solidity, and dogmatism of that adamant pastor, whose name is legion. It has a loosening, liberating effect. Yet at the same time it teaches a lesson of precision and emphasizes recourse to tradition in a way and to a degree that previous paradigms have not. The usual view has been that recourse to tradition guarantees truth, for it assures continuity with the revealed word of God himself, who can neither deceive nor be deceived, and therefore will not deceive us. Nor talk nonsense. There is the new point, revealed by our paradigm. It is only the fact of revelation which establishes the *meaningfulness* of the more transcendent mysteries of Christian faith. A description of scarlet by a blind man is as likely to be incoherent and meaningless as it is to be false. A doctrine such as that of the Holy Trinity or the Eucharist, ventured by a mere man, would stand an equal chance of not even making sense.

Hence, too, the need for precision, both in determining the original message and in preserving it. We cannot be too scientific in determining as accurately as possible the words used, their Greek or Aramaic meanings, their use in contemporary literature, the proximate setting and general background of Christ's statements, the mentality of those he addressed, the effect his words actually produced—anything which permits us to

put ourselves in a position equivalent to that of the blind man
who, in a familiar setting, with people he knows, hears familiar
words combined in this new, apt way: "Scarlet is like a trumpet note." Those English words, to him, in the context of his
question,[7] are the very best ones. Time may pass, concepts may
shift, whole languages may appear and disappear, circumstances may alter radically; but if we would learn what the
blind man learned and transmit it, we must go back to the
beginning, then take all these developments into account, before attempting to reformulate the doctrine in different words
and in a very different setting.

Contrast this paradigm with the familiar one of *via positiva,
via negativa,* and *via eminentiae.* This traditional scheme
(whose basic validity I have defended in Chapter Two) is calculated to give the impression that our terms are all so approximate when used to designate divine realities that it cannot matter too much which ones we use. The paradigm of the blind
man corrects this impression. It is precisely *because* their reference is so transcendent that hardly any other words will do.
Many things resemble a trumpet note in many ways, but only a
few of them are similarly suggestive of scarlet, and still fewer
could be used in place of a trumpet note in the description of
scarlet. And of course the blind man does not know which they
are, and has no way of telling. If he would hold on to his transcendent truth, therefore, he must preserve the original words,
or at least the exact comparison.[8] He cannot play fast and
loose with the original form and still keep the content. The revelation is fragile, perishable, elusive. The very meaning of the
words will slip through a new verbal net more readily still than
would their truth in the common view I have mentioned.

In such cases as these, therefore, even were we to succeed in
being thoroughly scientific, we would have to recognize that we
are unprofitable servants. We have not added a thing, or im-
proved on the teaching of Christ. It is as transcendent and mysterious as ever. At best, if we have been careful and competent,
it may be almost as good as new. I would not speak in this

fashion of all doctrines or of all theological activity. But for transcendent mysteries—for revelation in the strongest sense—yes, this is the model I would follow. The prevalent perspective, though, has been so dissimilar that I considered this another important reason for writing: the defense of mystery.

Ecumenical Implications

Mystery has need of protection, notice, from heterodox and orthodox alike. Think, for instance, of the way an avant-garde theologian and his opponents, denying and defending some mystery, may proceed with the same mistaken sureness about meaning as we observed in the pastor and his parishioner. The progressive theologian, in the sort of exchange I am imagining, rejects with assurance, yet rejects he knows not what. He says perhaps that Christ is not really present in the Eucharist, as though he knew just what it meant for Christ to be really present and had seen it wasn't so. His opponents, for their part, perhaps reveal a basically similar attitude, seeing nothing extraordinary in the denial but merely a sad mistake. They do not ask in amazement: "Have you had a vision, then, which showed you just how things are? Did you behold the heavens opened, and there on one side the transcendent meaning of the doctrine and on the other side the divine reality, and did you compare the two? Did you intuit the precise meaning of 'This is my body' and recognize the impossibility of capturing even part of that mystery with the words 'real presence'? If not, how can you be so sure that Christ is not really present in the Eucharist? What are you denying, and what do you suppose was being said?" In other cases there may not even be such parity in error; the label "orthodoxy" may in fact be claimed by a rationalism which is even more opposed to the revealed mystery than is skepticism about the rationalist version.

Such observations are relevant to the growing dialog between Christians of various denominations, divided by doctrinal divergencies which many consider the chief obstacle to Christian unity. In their efforts to resolve these differences, theologians have become ever more aware that disagreement may be only apparent, or less profound than differences in emphasis and terminology may suggest. Accordingly, they have been careful to look beneath mere formulae and not to be duped by appearances. It might seem, therefore, that the only effect of a study like the present one would be still greater interest and perhaps greater competence in a direction already taken. But I would expect the effect to be more radical, and not a mere matter of degree, first because of the step from the distinction of senses to the distinction of language-games, and second because of the step from asking what the meaning is to asking whether there is one. These are the two points I shall discuss, within this ecumenical context.

First, with regard to the way meaning has been studied, notice that the scholastic theologians who formulated so many "theories" concerning the Eucharist were, in a sense, sticklers for meaning. They defined their terms, then distinguished and sub-distinguished. But they were in the dark, for the most part, about their language-game. They did not dig into depth grammar. And it is my general impression that despite certain changes in tone and attitude, in this respect little has changed. And that is not surprising. For the same is true even in philosophy. Analytic and linguistic philosophers have been slow to assimilate the most revolutionary and consequential aspect of Wittgenstein's later philosophy, namely his insistence that the philosopher become reflectively aware and critical of his own language-game: what he is doing and why, according to what rules, based on what presuppositions and expectations and tacit agreements.[9] Hence many continue to do philosophy as Wittgenstein did in his "scientific" youth, before he came to understand the impossibility of such an approach. Theologians, too, I feel, have much the same lesson to learn. If they do, rather dramatic developments may result in ecumenical dialogue. Some barriers may dissolve.

To illustrate briefly and in broad outline the more radical approach I have in mind, I shall return to the discussion of the Eucharist already initiated in the previous section. What, in this case, are the major presuppositions to keep clearly in mind during theological reflection? I think they are chiefly two: (1) The words Christ spoke to his followers were meaningful, true, and apt; (2) if so, they expressed a transcendent reality. To take bread in his hands, give it to them, and say, "This is my body which is offered up for you," was not a familiar form of speech, to express a familiar idea. It *could* have been merely poetic. But to leave it at that and offer no explanation, when an intelligible translation was feasible, would have been misleading. Witness the belief of Christians from the start. So this seems a firm basis from which Christian theologians may work: whatever truth the words express, it is beyond our reach.

Now, what norms does this latter presupposition set for subsequent theologizing? Clearly this chief one: we must not seek to resolve the mystery. We must always keep this prime principle in mind: we are the blind, he is the one who sees. This means that we should neither try to bring the Eucharist completely down to our level so as to render it fully intelligible, nor, on the other hand, seek to explain or clarify the mystery through recourse to transcendent metaphysics. The former tendency has elicited some of the Church's sharpest reactions; the latter she has been far less alert to. The time has come, I suggest, for Catholic theologians to realize more clearly than they have till now that nothing they say in explanation can add to the two simple points I enunciated at the start: (1) The words of Christ expressed perfectly (2) something no other man could know or express. If you *translate* his words faithfully, as in competent modern versions of the New Testament, and fully indicate their context, you capture the whole message. You have it all—the whole mystery: real presence, trans-substantiation, and the rest. As I explained previously, insofar as these doctrines are both meaningful and true, they owe it to their derivation from Christ's own words. But there is no guarantee that the later formulations are as apt as his. The chances are they are not. Think once more of the blind man, and of the likelihood that he could improve on or even match the sighted man's words, "Scarlet is like a trumpet note."

The upshot for ecumenical discussion is that the parties in dialog need merely agree on the two basic suppositions I have mentioned. And there should be little difficulty about that. Any Christian believing in a divine revelation through Jesus Christ need only extend that general attitude to the Eucharist, and accept Christ's words as a divine, therefore meaningful, true, and apt expression of a divine and therefore transcendent reality.[10] Having accepted this much, he will have accepted all the meaning and truth contained in subsequent magisterial expressions of that original message. And having rejected a reductionist naturalism, he will have rejected the basic error the magisterium has sought to counteract in insisting on a real and not a merely figurative presence, or on transubstantiation and not, say, a type of transignification which would void Christ's gift of mystery and, by implication, suggest that his mode of expression was needlessly obscure. We cannot do better than he.

The usual attitude, simply put, is that the Church, which authored Scripture, must also interpret it, and that the prime requisite for doctrinal agreement is acceptance of the Church's interpretation. Now reflection on the notable differences between various doctrines alerts us to corresponding differences in the meaning of "interpretation", when applied in one case or the other. The language-game varies. In the present instance, examination of the epistemological situation suggests that it would be more accurate to say that the words of Christ clarify the words of the magisterium, rather than the other way round. The "interpretation" needs interpreting more than do the words interpreted, which in fact provide the best and only ultimate explanation of the magisterial statements. If we would understand what "real presence" means, or "transubstantiation", we must consult Christ, not the metaphysicians. His words are the best gloss of all. And if we are tempted to ask for their meaning too, the answer is: "There is no better expression for this reality." We must know where to stop: at mystery.

For the sake of overall clarity, I have not spelled out this position with the care its boldness requires.[11] I leave the necessary distinctions to the reader and refer him back, for a somewhat fuller indication of my meaning, to previous discussions both of the blind-man paradigm, in Chapters Two and Four, and of the Eucharist, in the preceding section of this chapter. Here my only purpose has been to suggest, through a single example, the kind of ecumenical openings which may result from the more radical type of analysis I have recommended and have tried to exemplify in these pages.

Doctrinal differences, I noted at the start, are regarded by many as the chief obstacle to Christian unity. But it might also be said that the great stumbling block is the divergent manner in which doctrinal questions are decided. After contrasting the Catholic approach with the Protestant, Walgrave remarks: "As long as man is man, the Catholic rule will involve the danger of oppression and abuse of authority, but the Protestant rule will always involve the danger of dissolution and arbitrary private judgment. This should be recognized by both parties, and mutual understanding on that point should be a basic condition of a real communion in the same living faith."[12] Faced with such a dichotomy, one naturally wonders how the conflicting values are to be reconciled. Is there not some ideal synthesis in which they may be united peacefully, the lion with the lamb? My preceding remarks suggest one possible, at least partial answer within the Catholic community: a rule of truth which is not a rule of meaning, and is recognized not to be.

Such a synthesis, fully assimilated, would represent a major step towards rapprochement with the non-Christian east, whose people form the majority of mankind. To the Western mind eastern religion has seemed mystic, nebulous, unrational; and naturally those of the East have had just the opposite impression of western religious thought. The Catholic tradition in particular, and especially scholastic theology, must appear strangely rationalistic to many an easterner. Were Catholic theologians to fully recognize the mystery in Christian revelation, in practice as well as in theory, much of this strangeness would disappear. However, if not clearly motivated, stress on mystery may appear to surrender a central value in western culture. And those who downgrade the cognitive or translate transcendence into moral categories do not thereby rejoin the mystic, contemplative traditions of the East. The solution is to be so completely faithful to the western, rational tradition that mystery finally receives its due. Theologians have long recognized the necessity of analogy; let them now note its implications.

I come now to my second main point concerning the ecumenical significance of this study. Since illustrations and explanations have already been provided, I can state it more briefly: a whole new dimension in ecumenical dialog opens up if the thesis of this book be admitted. It may be that in this or that case a doctrinal conflict can be resolved, not by admitting error on one side or the other, or by reconciling the senses of conflicting formulations, but by recognizing that one or the other formula, as it stands, is ultimately incoherent or void of meaning. The preceding study of *Casti Connubii* has shown, I trust, that this is not a farfetched hypothesis. The question of contraception has, in fact, been a major point of disagreement among Christians (the encyclical, for example, was a response to Lambeth), and the conflict would be resolved if it appeared, after further study, that the tentative conclusion of my analysis is roughly accurate.

Crisis in Ethics

The contraception issue is just one example, typical of a general trend in Catholic, Christian, and indeed western moral thought down through the ages. On the one hand there is the tendency to absolutize precepts (by which I here mean statements, not commands), making the morality of a defined action independent of the varying circumstances in which it is performed. On the other hand there is an equally strong tendency to relate the precept to value and take the related values and disvalues as absolutes. Thus moralists have been wont to say simply that this or that action is wrong, much as one might say this or that substance is heavy, without regard for circumstances and often without even considering the possibility that an action so defined might be wrong in one situation but not in another. But they have also been wont to justify their judgments by citing consequences or noting aspects of the action not mentioned in its definition. And from the fact that the argument ends there, one can see that such consequences or such aspects are absolutes. Pain, hunger, mutilation, loss of life, fear, destruction of property, ignorance, estrangement and endless other items are *never* reasons for performing an action. Life, health, happiness, peace, and many other items are *always* pluses. Now the great question for Christian morality is whether a system can coherently combine both these absolutes —absolute precepts (in the sense of statements) with absolute values and disvalues. And if it cannot, then I think it is clear which must go. With other moral issues already threatening on the horizon or breaking at this moment, it is imperative that clarity be introduced into the discussion—imperative so as to avoid further crises within the Church, imperative so as to remove or lessen this major source of friction between different Christian communities.

I suspect, in fact, that the number-one theological issue of the day may be whether the first sort of absoluteness, that of precepts, does or can characterize the authentic teaching of Christ, either in the Church today or in the initial revelation entrusted to her care. If the hypothesis is not meaningful, if it does not make sense to specify an action in abstract terms, then declare that any concrete action satisfying the description is morally wrong, regardless of circumstances, then no such thing has been revealed, and the issue can be settled analytically without any other recourse to Scripture and tradition than that required to determine the relevant, Christian sense of "wrong". This seems, in fact, to be the most practical way to put the problem in focus, and the most promising road to a solution. For it is not possible to initiate a historical inquiry without first answering the question of meaning. It is not possible, that is, to determine whether and in what sense a doctrine is revealed, nor how it is connected with the words of Christ, nor the weight it should therefore be given, without first divining the doctrine beneath the particular set of words—and whether there is one.

Wider Ecumenism

High on the list of my motives for writing there figured as well the original inspiration of this book, which has lost none of its force. The thought used to occur to me that I should write an article bearing some such title as "Theology in a New Key". The message would be that theologians do not realize all that linguistic philosophy has to offer. True, they recognize that it will help with language, and that language is important. But linguistic philosophy is not simply the philosophy of language, any more than dialectical philosophy is the philosophy of dialectic, or Kantian philosophy is the study of Kant.[13] The "linguistic turn" has introduced a new *way* of doing philosophy, for reasons which apply equally to theology. Thus would the abstract exhortation go. However, the readers of such an article might well remark that the proof of the pudding is the eating. So here, instead of the sermon, is a sample serving.

Thus this whole study, in which I have made such frequent use of the method of models, is itself a sort of Wittgensteinian language-game, illustrating through a single case, fully developed, the kind of relevance linguistic, analytic thought can have for theology. Linguistic philosophy raises new, important questions; introduces new techniques for dealing with them; offers new solutions, of a different kind, for old conundrums. The situation verifies René D'Ouince's description: "A new 'problematic' in a given area of knowledge brings out an aspect of reality which had not yet been clearly perceived nor formally expressed. It usually provokes a certain revision of all that had previously been acquired or, to speak more accurately, it reveals, not the inaccuracy, but the inadequacy of prior systematisations. The relative importance of questions shifts, and the interest taken in them by the men of a generation."[14]

A "revision of all that had previously been acquired" is a risky business. Hence the Church and her theologians are repeatedly faced by the alternative described in the parable of the talents, whose relevance at the moment of its utterance C. H. Dodd suggests as follows: " 'The Judaism of that time,' says Dr. Klausner, 'had no other aim than to save the tiny nation, the guardian of great ideals, from sinking into the broad sea of heathen culture.' Put that way, it seems a legitimate aim. But from another point of view, might it not be aptly described as hiding the treasure in a napkin? To abandon the scrupulous discipline of Pharisaism would be a risk, no doubt. It was precisely the risk that the early Christians took, and they took it under the inspiration of their Master. It is the kind of risk, this parable suggests, that all investment of capital involves; but without the risk of investment the capital remains barren. We have here, it seems, a pointed application of the parable which arises directly out of the historical situation."[15]

The application can be made to many a subsequent situation. The natural temptation of anyone entrusted with a divine deposit is to store it up carefully and run no risks. And the risks of contamination always seem proportionately greater the more pagan the population with which one must mix. So the over-careful custodian may easily fail to notice or recall that the world's pagans are the intended recipients of the treasure entrusted to him, and that the Master expects an investment, and expects it most of all where the danger seems greatest.

St. Thomas understood this. The great pagan threat of the Middle Ages was Aristotle. Not mere ignorance of his thought or mistrust of the new and strangemade popes, bishops and theologians so fearful of his influence that they forbade the use of his works. No, it was evident that on fundamental points Aristotle's views were incompatible with Christian faith. The danger was increased by the superiority of his thought, and its consequent prestige. The risks of dialog with such a partner appeared all too plainly in the Averroists and their doctrine of double truth. The only truly Christian response to such a challenge, many therefore felt, was resistance. As far as possible, Aristotle was to be ignored, and students had to be isolated from contact with his thought. Others, more competent, might take a look at his writings, so as to combat and refute them, but not to enter into genuine dialog with him or to learn anything from a pagan. The treasure of Christian faith had to be kept tightly wrapped in its napkin.

Such was not Aquinas's attitude. With deeper faith, understanding, and courage, he ventured into that pagan world of thought, despite its dangers. He read Aristotle, studied him, became his disciple. But, as we now put it, he also baptized him. Because he genuinely entered into the Stagyrite's thought and made much of it his own, he was capable of the great synthesis which resolved the crisis. Of course, that is not how many of his contemporaries saw his achievement. Some called him a heretic and bishops condemned his theses.

Such well-intentioned short-sightedness is predictable. Consider the case of Teilhard. Once again a current of thought arose from without the Church, acquired immense prestige and influence, and seemed to threaten Christian belief, for the same reasons as before. For one thing, ignorance of evolutionary science rendered most theologians and Christian thinkers incapable of an accurate evaluation. For another, the challenge was new and required serious examination of questions for which no ready-made answers were available. And there was no telling where one might end if the evolutionary thesis were accepted. Furthermore, it was clear that many of these scientists were "pagan"—non-Christians—and that many of their assertions were in direct conflict with Christian faith. Who was to tell whether the errors were separable from the more scientific tenets, and whether acceptance of part would not lead inevitably to acceptance of too much and to the loss of the precious deposit entrusted by Christ to the care of his Church? Better to wrap it up tight—and to keep people from reading the works of anyone who attempted to follow the example of St. Thomas and mediate the message of Christ to the gentiles. For in any such pioneering attempt, errors are likely to be committed. So beware of Teilhard!

A similar situation now exists with regard to analytic philosophy. It is the dominant philosophical trend in English-speaking lands, and enjoys great prestige, but is little known by Catholic thinkers, and is mistrusted by many of them, for the familiar reasons. For one thing, their lack of acquaintance with analytic thought permits the grossest misunderstandings. And uncertainty about the implications of various analytic or linguistic tenets adds to the fears born of these misunderstandings. In addition, analytic philosophy, like much evolutionary thought and Aristotelian philosophy before it, is pagan property, produced and practiced by non-Christians, even anti-Christians, whose views frequently conflict with Christian doctrine. But both the good of the Church and the good of the gentiles require that this gap, too, be bridged. In many circles, the Christian message will not be accepted or understood if those who present it are incapable of analytic discussion and dialogue, or reveal the same sort of total antipathy towards analytic thinking which some Augustinians felt towards Aristotle and many Victorians showed towards Darwin. The modern custodian of the gospel for whom analytic and linguistic thought is simply "positivism" or "rationalism" may wrap the gospel so tight it is invisible to all but its possessor. And the theologian who merely acknowledges the possibility or presence of certain values in the analytic tradition, while comfortably sure that the same values are abundantly present in his own, has made no investment and will reap no profit. For that it is necessary to imitate Thomas and Teilhard and recognize that the gentiles have something of their own to offer, of great and genuine value. Not just "our separated brethren", but our separated brothers—not just Luther but Wittgenstein. Christian thought may then be swelled by still another tributary, and continue to mirror in its growth the process by which the Christian community grows, through the accretion of ever new peoples, inhabiting continents unknown to the apostles. Having ventured anew, through missionaries of the mind, into dangerous heathen lands, Christendom may once again have reason to say:

> And he brought forth his people with joy,
> His chosen ones with joyous song.
> And he gave them the lands of the nations;
> Of the toil of the peoples they took possession,
> That they might keep his statutes
> And observe his laws. (Ps. 105)

Notes

PREFACE

    1. *Unfolding Revelation. The Nature of Doctrinal Development* (London-Philadelphia, 1972), pp. 153-54.

CHAPTER ONE

    1. *Pragmatism* (New York, 1928), p. 73 (in italics).
    2. *The Varieties of Religious Experience* (New York, 1902), p. 445.
    3. Besides, what is the relevance of relevance? "Is the potter of no more account than the clay?" (Is. 29, 16)
    4. *Pragmatism*, p. 50.
    5. "Intrinsèquement déshonnête," in P. Delhaye, J. Grootaers and G. Thils: *Pour Relire Humanae Vitae* (Gembloux, 1970).
    6. *Ibid.*, p. 26.
    7. *Ibid.*, p. 27.
    8. *Ibid.*, p. 30.
    9. *Philosophical Investigations*, trans. by G. E. M. Anscombe, 2d ed. (Oxford, 1967), §307. The frequency of my subsequent references to the later Wittgenstein calls for explanation. He would surely have rejected my whole enterprise, reflecting as it does an interest in doctrinal statements and belief that they have important cognitive content. Yet despite his restricted views of philosophy, theology and religion, which I do not share, I feel that when properly understood he has more to offer in a discussion like the present one than any other thinker I know.
    10. Wittgenstein's is best known. Cf. *e.g., Investigations*, §§661-693.
    11. Number 649 of Wittgenstein's *On Certainty* (Oxford, 1969), where he is making a different point, provides an equally apt illustration: "I once said to someone—in English—that the shape of a certain branch was typical of the branch of an elm, which my companion denied. Then we came past some ashes, and I said 'There, you see, here are the branches I was speaking about.' To which he replied 'But that's an ash'—and I said 'I always meant ash when I said elm.' "
    12. *The Blue and Brown Books* (Oxford, 1960), p. 17.
    13. *Investigations*, §130.
    14. *Confessions*, XI, 29.
    15. "Religious Assertions and Doctrinal Development," *Theological Studies*, 27 (1966), pp. 531-32.

CHAPTER TWO

1. Wittgenstein, *Investigations*, §96.
2. *Ibid.*, §66.
3. *Ibid.*, §67.
4. *Ibid.*, §396.
5. *Ibid.*, §69.
6. *Ibid.*, §524.
7. *Ibid.*, p. 216.
8. *Ibid.*
9. *Ibid.*, p. 204.
10. *The Blue and Brown Books*, pp. 129-30.
11. *Ibid.*, pp. 8-9.

CHAPTER THREE

1. Ayer's emotive theory is much more categorical than recent, more influential versions; that is why I have chosen it, for dialectical clarity, before my own attempt at synthesis.
2. Second edition (London, 1946), p. 108.
3. *Ibid.*, p. 107.
4. *Remarks on the Foundations of Mathematics*, trans. by G. E. M. Anscombe (Oxford, 1956), p. 54.
5. *Zettel*, trans. by G. E. M. Anscombe (Oxford, 1967), §173.
6. *Investigations*, p. 174.
7. *Zettel*, §488.
8. *Investigations*, §476.
9. "Intention," *Proceedings of the Aristotelian Society*, 57 (1956-57), p. 323.
10. In Wittgenstein's familiar terminology, which I am employing here, "surface grammar" is "what immediately impresses itself upon us about the use of a word," "the way it is used in the construction of the sentence, the part of its use—one might say—that can be taken in by the ear" (*Investigations*, §664). "Depth grammar", on the other hand, is far more difficult to discern (*ibid.*); "we do not *command a clear view* of the use of our words" (*ibid.*, §122), of "the game with these words, their employment in the linguistic intercourse that is carried on by their means" (*ibid.*, §182).
11. John Dewey, *Experience and Nature* (New York, 1929), p. 108.
12. *Investigations*, §§354-6. That Wittgenstein himself envisaged an application such as I shall make, in the realm of ethics, appears from G. E. Moore's notes on "Wittgenstein's Lectures in 1930-33," in *Philosophical Papers* (London, 1959), p. 313.
13. See Wittgenstein, *On Certainty*, trans. by D. Paul and G. E. M. Anscombe (Oxford, 1969), §402.
14. Cf. the contrasting perspectives analyzed at the end of this chapter.
15. Charles L. Stevenson, *Ethics and Language* (New Haven, 1944), p. 3.
16. *Zettel*, §455.
17. Thus the present observations are no more damaging for the objectivity of ethical statements (in the sense of objectivity just discussed) than would be similar remarks concerning, say, the difficulty a modern scientist

might experience in understanding Galileo, especially if he spoke in Latin.

18. Despite (and in part because of) the modifier "moral", Duncan Derrett's warning is opportune: "In the Anglo-Saxon world one hears emphasis upon the quite mistaken notion that Christ's teaching was anti-law, and that Christ came to free men from law. Away with the letter, and back to the spirit! This is folly. Christ in fact interpreted the *Torah*, the Jewish corpus of law, in ways which were intellectually possible, by methods intellectually viable—if often with inconvenient implications. The notion that his coming meant the end of law and of legal thinking is false" (*Law in the New Testament*, London, 1970, p. xxvi). However, contrast Jesus' attitude, as "master of the Sabbath", with the mentality Derrett describes: "What God demands is good, but this is to be done not because it is good but because God demands it. This curious notion, which Jews share with Muslims, appeals to a mind which accepts paternal authority without question; and this point must not be lost sight of, since the myth that the Jews were bowed down under a sombre and joyless weight of perhaps as many as six hundred and thirteen commandments enforced by an authoritarian deity has been widely misunderstood in the interests of Christian apologetics. . . .the emotional satisfaction of having kept on the right side of the requirements of a super-Father, of having obtained the approval of the chief prestige-holder in an intensely self-absorbed hierarchical society, was a positive and even a beautiful sensation, which the ritualists exploit not as conscious confidence-tricksters but as purveyors of a commodity which was in general demand" (*Ibid.*, xxii-xxiii).

CHAPTER FOUR

1. See Chapter Two, #6.

2. A. Flew and A. Macintyre (eds.), *New Essays in Philosophical Theology* (London, 1969), pp. 98-99.

3. *Ibid.*

4. *Ibid.*, p. 106.

5. If contemporary physicists see more clearly than the rest of us that there is and can be no such definitive block in this particular case, they may readily imagine proposals farther out on the horizons of science, where the possibility of ultimate incompatibility might arise. I could then make the same remarks about those proposals.

6. *Ludwig Wittgenstein. A Memoir* (London, 1962), pp. 65-66.

7. *The Church Teaches. Documents of the Church in English Translation* (St. Louis, 1960), p. 137.

8. *De Castitate et de Vitiis Contrariis Tractatus Doctrinalis et Moralis*, 2d ed. (Rome, 1921), p. xi.

9. In his treatment there is no balancing of values and disvalues, as in the discussion of many other precepts even within the natural-law tradition.

10. *Op. cit.*, p. 255.

11. *Ibid.*

12. *Ibid.*, pp. 225, 239-40, 249.

13. *Ibid.*, p. 257.

14. *Ibid.*, pp. 239, 257.

15. *Summa Theologica*, Ia, q. 76, a. 1.

16. "It is not to be expected," writes one commentator revealingly, "that

we should find the proofs for the general theory of matter and form set forth in argumentative style in the writings of the Angelic Doctor, as we do in those of modern scholastics. In the thirteenth century hylemorphism as a general truth was unquestioned. Disagreement concerned the nature of matter and form, and the extent of their domain." Cf. B. Gerrity, *The Relations Between the Theory of Matter and Form and the Theory of Knowledge in the Philosophy of Saint Thomas Aquinas* (Washington, 1936), p. 8. When even truth is unquestioned, who will doubt meaning?

17. Gerrity continues in the same revealing vein: "The philosophers of the schools since the great period of the thirteenth century have likewise held firmly to this theory. As in the time of St. Thomas there have been differences in regard to the precise nature of primary matter and substantial form, details of the theory and applications of it, but to the proposition that all material things are compounded of an active determining principle, the form, and a passive determinable principle, the matter, the schoolmen have always remained faithful" (*ibid.*, p. 10). Their task, as they saw it, was to accurately describe an acknowledged entity or cogently prove its existence, not to establish meaning.

18. *Metaph.*, 1029 a 4-6.

19. St. Thomas, *In VII Metaphys.*, ii. Italics mine.

20. *Idem, In I Physic.*, lect. xiii, n. 9.

21. *Idem, Summa*, Ia, q. 70, a. 3, c.

22. *Ibid.*, q. 105, a. 1, c.

23. *La philosophie de s. Thomas d'Aquin*, nouvelle éd., t. 2 (Paris, 1940), pp. 7-8.

24. *Summa*, Ia, q. 76, a. 5.

25. *De Ente et Essentia*, 2a.

26. *Summa*, Ia, q. 44, a. 2.

27. *Investigations*, §164.

28. *Summa*, Ia, q. 77, a. 1, ad 7.

29. Cf. *e.g., Summa*, Ia, q. 3, a. 3, c.

30. *Ibid.*, q. 29, a. 2 ad 3.

31. *Pragmatism* (New York, 1928), pp. 201, 215-16.

32. *Ibid.*, p. 50.

33. *Ibid.*, p. 49.

34. "Pragmatism in Retrospect," in J. Buchler (ed.), *The Philosophy of Peirce. Selected Writings* (New York, 1940), p. 273.

35. Arthur Lovejoy, "What Is the Pragmaticist Theory of Meaning? The First Phase," in P. Wiener and F. Young (eds.), *Studies in the Philosophy of Charles Sanders Peirce* (Cambridge, Mass., 1952), p. 5.

CHAPTER FIVE

1. *Investigations*, p. 209.

2. L. Wittgenstein, *Tractatus Logico-Philosophicus*, trans. by D. F. Pears and B. F. McGuinness (London, 1961), 4.002.

3. See A. Maslow, *A Study in Wittgenstein's Tractatus* (Berkeley-London, 1961), p. x.

4. *Ibid.*

5. See, e.g., *Investigations*, §47.

6. *The Church Teaches*, p. 147.

7. For a recent survey of the literature, see T. Schneider, *Die Einheit des Menschen. Die anthropologische Formel "anima forma corporis" im sogenannten Korrektorienstreit und bei Petrus Johannis Olivi. Ein Beitrag zur Vorgeschichte des Konzils von Vienne* (Münster, 1972), pp. 215-22. On page 221, C. Partee is quoted as saying: "The precise aim of the decree was as obscure in this regard then as it is now, and each, as now, interpreted it according to his general attitude."

8. See *Revue des sciences ecclésiastiques*, 36 (1877), p. 86.

9. Henri Bouillard, "Notions conciliaires et Analogie de la Vérité," *Recherches de Science Religieuse*, 35 (1948), p. 262.

10. B. Jansen, "Quonam spectet definitio Concilii Viennensis de anima," *Gregorianum*, 1 (1920), p. 80.

11. *Op. cit.*, e.g., p. 252.

12. Cf. E. Müller, *Das Konzil von Vienne*, 1311-1312 (Münster, 1934), pp. 284-5.

13. Cf. Jansen, *op. cit.*, pp. 83-5.

14. For example, see Schneider, *op. cit.*, pp. 230, 235.

15. For remarks in this direction, see *ibid.*, pp. 251-2 (which, however, should be complemented by pp. 256-7, for a more accurate picture of Schneider's own view).

16. *Ibid.*, p. 252.

17. *Ibid.*

18. The translation is from John T. Noonan, Jr., *Contraception: A History of its Treatment by the Catholic Theologians and Canonists* (Cambridge, Mass., 1965), p. 427.

19. *Ibid.*, pp. 424-25.

20. See *ibid.*, p. 482.

21. *Ibid.*, p. 243. After a more thorough survey of Aquinas's teaching than seemed appropriate here, Noonan comments: "Did it make sense to postulate one type of coitus as normal, and to treat every variation from it as accidental, even cases in which it was known that conception was impossible? Did it make sense to say that old age was an 'accidental' exception to the ability to generate? Thomas did not ask these questions."

22. See Chapter Four, #5.

23. See the discussion in Chapter Three.

24. Again, see Chapter Three, for some preliminary suggestions.

25. It is immaterial here whether this imagined exchange be historical or complete. It suffices that it be representative of moral argumentation; and the passages from Old and New Testament cited in Chapter Three show that it is. I am returning to the method of language-games, already explained.

26. Since this may be largely uncharted territory for some readers, let me mention that evidence of value-oriented thinking elsewhere in rabbinic literature, with regard to some other obligation, would not force a reassessment in this case. Shifts of meaning from context to context, for one and the same person, are as common as changes in the weather. We speak, for example, of deep blue, deep concern, deep meaning, a deep well, and deep notes; of a high price, a high tower, and high spirits; of a sharp cry, a sharp knife, and a sharp dispute; etc. It would be perverse to say the meaning must be constant since we use the same word. It would be equally and similarly mistaken to argue (though the conclusion might by accident be true) that since the author

of the encyclical elsewhere calculated values and disvalues in reaching a moral verdict, such must be the thinking behind the condemnation of contraception, and such its meaning.

27. *Reflections on the Psalms* (London, 1958), p. 112.

CHAPTER SIX

1. Lawrence F. Barmann, *Baron Friedrich von Hügel and the Modernist Crisis in England* (Cambridge, 1972), p. 98.

2. The following remarks on conversion to the metric system provide an apt comparison, point by point, in fact a sort of allegory: "An estimate of the total cost of conversion is impossible to compute, but the costs and inconveniences involved would be temporary—they would stop at the end of the transition period. The benefits would continue indefinitely. With the haphazard adoption now in progress, moreover, it might take 50 years to get things straightened out. . . ." ("Here Comes the Meter!", *Reader's Digest*, April 1972)

3. *An Essay on the Development of Christian Doctrine*, second ed. (London, 1906), p. 362.

4. *Lectures and Conversations on Aesthetics, Psychology and Religious Belief*, ed. by C. Barrett (Oxford, 1966), p. 2.

5. Since I have followed Wittgenstein on so many points and so may be thought to be presenting a Wittgensteinian view of doctrinal statements, let me recall that his attitude towards dogma and dogmatic theology was negative. For him, religious belief was "an attitude" (Man. 169), "a trust" (Man. 168, p. 2). [The references are to unpublished manuscripts listed in G. H. von Wright, "The Wittgenstein Papers," *Philosophical Review*, 78 (1969), pp. 483-503.] Between no theology and the kind of theology often objected to, I would favor this mean: a theology which recognizes mystery in practice as well as in theory.

6. Chapter Two, #7.

7. Again, see Chapter Two, #7.

8. Notice that a saving connection with apostolic teaching was missing in both the cases in which I gave a negative judgment in Chapter Five, whereas it was the plausibility of such a connection which assured the meaningfulness of the trinitarian formulae in Chapter Four.

9. See the final case study in Chapter Four.

10. This they can be regardless of whether they were statements of fact or, say, ritual formulae. Practically all types of expression, including liturgical ones, reveal convictions and convey information. It would be a blunder, no doubt, to suppose that the words, "We praise thee, Father, for thy great kindness," report an activity being performed; but it would be equally mistaken to suppose that they express nothing of the speaker's or community's beliefs about God and his providence.

11. I have found, for instance, that it is necessary to point out the following fairly obvious fact: the Church might nevertheless clarify even these texts in important ways, connecting them with others, putting them in context, ruling out reductive readings. But none of this is the same as replacing the words of Christ with supposedly clearer formulae. The words of Vatican I affirming the Church's role as interpreter of Scripture (DS 3007) do not imply

that she is capable of clarifying each individual passage in every one of the ways in which any text might conceivably be clarified.

12. *Unfolding Revelation*, p. 189.

13. On pp. 11-12 of his *Critique of Linguistic Philosophy* (Oxford, 1970), C. Mundle expresses a typical viewpoint: "*Whatever others may have meant by 'linguistic philosophy', I am using it, appropriately I think, to refer to philosophers' writings which assert or assume that the subject-matter of philosophy is language, or the uses of words (or of language), or grammar, or concepts if talk about 'concepts' turns out, as it commonly does, to be talk about the uses of words. Linguistic philosophy, in this sense, is now widespread in English-speaking countries.*" Of course Mundle means that language is considered the *only* matter of philosophy, and thus understood the description fits some linguistic philosophers but not others, and in any case hardly does justice to the possibilities and intrinsic significance of linguistic philosophy.

14. *Un Prophète en Procès: Teilhard de Chardin et L'Avenir de la Pensée Chrétienne* (Paris, 1970), p. 15.

15. *The Parables of the Kingdom* (London, 1936), p. 152.